Duquesne Studies - Philological

Series 6

STERNE'S COMEDY

A Modern Humanities Research Association

Monograph

A

MODERN HUMANITIES

RESEARCH ASSOCIATION MONOGRAPH

Duquesne Studies Philological Series

6

STERNE'S COMEDY OF MORAL SENTIMENTS: THE ETHICAL DIMENSION OF THE *JOURNEY*

by
ARTHUR HILL CASH

Foreword by HERBERT READ

DUQUESNE UNIVERSITY PRESS,
Pittsburgh, Pa.

Editions E. Nauwelaerts, Louvain, Belgium

The *Modern Humanities Research Association*

Monograph Committee

Library of Congress Catalog Card Number 65-13007

DUQUESNE STUDIES

PHILOLOGICAL SERIES

For my wife

L'amour n'est *rien* sans sentiment.

Et le sentiment est encore *moins* sans amour.

ACKNOWLEDGMENT

It gives me pleasure to acknowledge my debt to the three teachers and scholars under whose guidance the original version of this study was prepared. I want to thank James Lowry Clifford for his patient direction of the research and his unflagging encouragement, Marjorie Hope Nicolson for her excellent suggestions and her persistent discouragement of my digressions, and Allen Tracy Hazen for his understanding counsel and painstaking criticism.

I am grateful to Sir Herbert for the stimulation of his insights and his generosity in writing the Foreword.

I am especially indebted to three friends. Richard Clark Tobias read and commented upon the typescript, and Rollo Fogarty proofed the final pages. I owe much to Forrest Williams for our many discussions of ethics and religion.

My thanks also to my colleagues, Julia Matott, for translating Jean Paul Richter; Morris Nellermoe, for consulting on Sterne's odd French; and John Sorbie, for designing the title page. I appreciate the cheerful help of the library staffs at Colorado State University and the University of Colorado.

I take this occasion to thank Donald Frederick Bond, whose teaching of Sterne set me upon the chain of inquiries which resulted eventually in this study.

A. H. C.
Colorado State University
October 30, 1965

FOREWORD

Laurence Sterne had the misfortune to be born an Englishman and to become a clergyman; both circumstances led to a misunderstanding of his sense of humour. The misunderstanding began in his own life-time and has continued until today. There is perhaps some excuse for not wishing to associate a sense of humour with a priestly calling, and the Church of England, to which Sterne belonged, has always maintained its puritanical sense of clerical dignity. But there is less excuse for those literary critics and conceited moralists whose only aim has been to suppress a frivolity they cannot share. Not that Sterne is frivolous, if to be frivolous is to be trivial or insincere. Sterne, like Rabelais and Shakespeare before him, uses frivolity for a serious purpose, which I take to be the revelation of our human nature. That 'nature' is very complex, and the more serious our study of it becomes (as in modern psychology) the more it seems to elude our grasp. Sterne's method, like Shakespeare's, was naturalistic—seeing humanity as an integral part of nature itself, nature with all its indifference to our moral rectitude.

And yet Sterne was himself a moralist, if by morals we mean, not moral laws but the principles that should guide human relations towards happiness. In that sense Sterne was a great moralist and the new meaning he gave to words like 'sentiment' and 'sensibility' brought the world to a better understanding of the springs of our actions. His peculiar humour proceeds from a subtle interchange of gesture and feeling, of thought and action, of speech and image, combining these into something so distinctive and yet so elusive that we cease to compare Sterne with Rabelais or Shakespeare, and look forward to the disciples he has had in every land—to Jean Paul Richter, Pushkin, Gogol, Joyce, Borges, Günther Grass.

All this is appreciated by Mr. Cash in this learned yet lively book which carries the rehabilitation of Sterne a stage farther. Some years ago I suggested that the *Sermons* should not be neglected in any attempt to present the true character of Sterne, and that is one of the original features of Mr. Cash's critical method. He has realized that the novels and the sermons have the same 'ethical dimension', and that Sterne was engaged upon a comedy of manners that must comprise every aspect of our human destiny, save perhaps the final tragic vision. But he realizes that Sterne's wit has its own sublime effects, and as Goethe said: 'Whoever reads him feels himself lifted above the petty cares of the world. His humour is inimitable, and it is not every kind of humour that leaves the soul calm and serene'. Or as Sterne himself said in one of his sermons, quoted by Mr. Cash, 'the great business of man is the regulation of his spirit; the possession of such a frame and temper of mind, as will lead us peaceably through this world.' Benevolence is not a fashionable word today, but Mr. Cash, in expounding Sterne's use of it, gives a new relevance to its ethical significance, and what begins as a study of *A Sentimental Journey* ends by being a complete vindication of one of the world's greatest humanists.

Herbert Read

CONTENTS

A NOTE ON DOCUMENTATION

In this study, Laurence Sterne's novels, sermons, and letters are cited by short titles or by page numbers alone when reference to the title is superfluous. The following texts have been used:

Sentimental Journey: *A Sentimental Journey through France and Italy*. Introduction by Virginia Woolf. World's Classics edition. Oxford University Press, 1928.

Tristram Shandy: *The Life and Opinions of Tristram Shandy, Gentleman*. Edited by James Aiken Work. New York: Odyssey Press, 1940.

Sermons, Vols. I and II: *The Sermons of Mr. Yorick* and *Sermons by the Late Rev. Mr. Sterne*, collected and renumbered in *Complete Works and Life of Laurence Sterne*. Introduction by Wilbur L. Cross. New York: J. F. Taylor, 1904. 12 vols., the sermons bound as Vols. VI and VII. Re-issued by the Clonmel Society, 12 vols. bound as six with the same pagination throughout; the sermons bound as Vol. V.

Letters: *Letters of Laurence Sterne*. Edited by Lewis Perry Curtis. Oxford: Clarendon Press, 1935.

Journal to Eliza: Included in the *Letters*.

Two studies of Sterne are cited by author alone:

Cross: *Life and Times of Laurence Sterne*, by Wilbur L. Cross. Yale University Press, third edition, 1929.

Hammond: *Laurence Sterne's 'Sermons of Mr. Yorick,'* by Lansing Van der Heyden Hammond. Yale University Press, 1948.

In quoting Sterne and other eighteenth-century writers, I have taken the liberty of changing spelling, capital letters, and italic print to conform to modern usage.

INTRODUCTION

Laurence Sterne had a flair for indecorous humor. He told the story of a church dignitary who lost a hot chestnut through a breach of his breeches, another of a boy circumcised by a falling window sash. He wrote a satire upon pedantry featuring a man whose enormous nose takes on a phallic meaning, and a delicate account of a French lady's frankness in excusing herself from a coach.

Yet, in ten brief years as a professional writer, the Rev. Mr. Laurence Sterne acquired a reputation as the most masterful sentimentalist of English letters. Few can forget in *Tristram Shandy* the indestructible love which binds the two elderly Shandy brothers, the kindness of Uncle Toby to a fly, or that inspired tale of a benevolent man's concern for a fellow in distress—the story of Le Fever. In *A Sentimental Journey*, Sterne's second and final novel, he reached the pinnacle of sentimentalism. This little, fictionalized travel-book, the primary concern of my present study, gave to the world some of its most famous stories—the caged starling which had been taught to cry, "I can't get out! I can't get out!"; Yorick's insult to a mendicant Franciscan which ends in a sympathetic exchange of snuff boxes; and a tender interview with a beautiful *paysanne*, driven mad with yearning for her lover.

Sterne's loose episodic narratives, which juxtaposed the sentimental scene with the coarse, invited critics to treat the author as a sort of schizophrenic anecdotist. The eighteenth- and nineteenth-century reviewers described by Alan B. Howes in *Yorick and the Critics*[1] admired Sterne's tenderness and sensibility, but most were blinded by their own prudishness. Ralph Griffiths, publisher of the *Monthly Review*, spoke for the majority when he accused Sterne of "bawdyisms" and "obscene asterisms!—setting the reader's imagination to work, and officiating as pimp to every lewd idea excited by your own creative abominable ambiguity." Yet in the same dialogue he praised Sterne as "a master in the science of human *feelings*," and commented that the story of Le Fever "has done you more honor than everything else you have wrote, except your Ser-

[1]Yale University Press, 1958.

17

mons." He went on to make a plea which was to become commonplace: "... excite our passions to *laudable* purposes—awake our
affections, engage our hearts—arouse, transport, refine, improve us.
Let morality, let the cultivation of virtue be your aim—let wit,
humor, elegance and pathos be the means; and the grateful applause
of mankind will be your reward."[2] Griffiths, who made his fortune
on the publication of "Fanny Hill" (John Cleland's *Memoirs of a
Woman of Pleasure*, 1749), might be expected to identify the moral
with the didactic. Unfortunately, many agreed: they could not see
Sterne's books as integral wholes, but thought of his indecencies as
fundamentally opposed to the sentimentalism.

The attacks brought no marked change in Sterne's method. To
be sure, he promised Bishop Warburton "that willingly and know-
ingly I will give no offense to any mortal by anything which I think
can look like the least violation either of decency or good manners."
A priest could hardly say anything else to his superior. But Sterne
was careful to add, "I may find it very hard, in writing such a book
as *Tristram Shandy*, to mutilate everything in it down to the prudish
humor of every particular. I will, however, do my best; though
laugh, my lord, I will, and as loud as I can too" (*Letters*, p. 115).

So throughout his life and most of the time since, critics attacked
his ribald wit, classing him with Samuel Butler, Rabelais, and Swift,
while in the next breath they praised his pathos, likening him to
Richardson, Rousseau, and Goethe. One group made of Sterne
what Herbert Ross Brown called "the high priest of the cult of
sensibility," gobbling up Tristram and Yorick truncated in *The
Beauties of Sterne; Including All His Pathetic Tales, and Most
Distinguished Observations on Life.* Another group fed on the resi-
due in joke books for men only, such as *Sterne's Witticisms, or
Yorick's Convivial Jester.* Thomas Jefferson regarded Sterne's works
as "the best course of morality that ever was written," but William
Makepeace Thackeray thought of him as a "foul satyr" whose eyes
"leer out of the leaves constantly."

A small minority, however, found in Sterne a picture of human
nature which embraced both good and evil. An unknown writer for
the *Critical Review* of January, 1762, seems to have begun a minor
tradition when he commented that if Sterne "sometimes lost sight
of Rabelais, he has directed his eye to a still greater original, even
nature herself."[3] As Alan Howes tells us, Joseph Cradock's com-

[2]*Monthly Review*, XXXII (February, 1765), 120-139.
[3]*Critical Review*, XIII (January, 1762), 68.

ment in *Village Memoirs* (1774) was frequently reprinted: "Sterne will be immortal when Rabelais and Cervantes are forgot—they drew their characters from the particular genius of the times—Sterne confined himself to nature only." In the following century, Hazlitt made what has become the most famous of all critical comments on Sterne: "My Uncle Toby is one of the finest compliments ever paid to human nature." Furthermore, Hazlitt ranked Sterne with Cervantes and the comic novelists of the eighteenth century, "the first-rate writers" who "take their rank by the side of reality, and are appealed to as evidence on all questions concerning human nature."[4]

Yet this praise of Sterne as an observer provided no aesthetic justification for his mixing of the pathetic with the indecent. Sterne's complete vindication evolved slowly among a few critics of unquestionable genius, but widely scattered in time and place, who saw Sterne, not as a wit, a Harlequin, or a jester, but as a "man of humor." Jean Paul Richter, in *Vorschule der Aesthetik*, 1804, began the tradition in Sterne criticism which, in my opinion, has been more rewarding than any other. His interpretation was closely followed by Samuel Taylor Coleridge. Then, in the late nineteenth century, Edmond Scherer, writing from the Sorbonne, fruitfully developed the ideas of Jean Paul, while in our own century Sir Herbert Read developed the comments of Coleridge. Scherer and Read wrote the complete justification of Sterne's mingled obscenity and sentimentalism.

Jean Paul ranked Sterne with Voltaire, Rabelais, Shakespeare, and Cervantes as a writer of "world humor" which is above petty attacks. The humorist sees a "totality" which embraces both the ridiculous (the finite small) and the sublime (the finite immense knowable only to the intellect), setting the two side by side. He may degrade the great or elevate the small, but his ultimate purpose is to destroy both "because everything is equal and nothing before the infinite." He sees the folly as well as the virtue of man, but from his transcendent view, both look small and vain. His laughter, however, is tolerant and melancholy, for he cannot deny that he personally is part of the foolish world.[5] Thus, without directly exonerating Sterne, Jean Paul

[4]*Complete Works*, ed. P.P. Howe (London and Toronto: J. M. Dent and Sons, 1930-34), Vol. XVI, 19; Vol. VI, 107. See also Vol. XVI, 6.

[5]*Vorschule der Aesthetik*, in *Jean Pauls Sämtliche Werke* (Weimar: Hermann Bönlaus Nachfolger, 1935), Abt. 1, Bd. 11, Chapters 26-33, pp. 93-119.

saw him in large terms which clearly implied that the charge of indecency was unjust.

Coleridge, in a lecture of 1818, acknowledged that he had taken certain key ideas from Jean Paul in his discussion of Sterne: "when we contemplate a finite in reference to the infinite, consciously or unconsciously, *humor* [arises]. So says Jean Paul Richter." "Humorous writers, therefore, as Sterne in particular, delight to end in nothing, or a direct contradiction." "In humor the little is made great, and the great little, in order to destroy both, because all is equal in contrast with the infinite." We might expect Coleridge to have looked upon the clashing bawdry and benevolence as the littleness and greatness of man which pale in the light of infinity. Indeed, his description of Sterne's naughtiness as the "white and black angels" of the mind suggests that very thing. Yet Coleridge understood Sterne's comedy, not as humor, but as wit, and wit which gives pain to modesty and triumphs over ignorance. Consequently, Sterne "cannot be too severely censured . . . for he makes the best dispositions of our nature the panders and condiments for the basest."[6]

Edmond Scherer, however, elaborating the views of Jean Paul, makes Sterne's fiction seem unified and complete. Although his essay, "Laurence Sterne, or the Humorist," is all but ignored by modern students, it is in my opinion the best explanation of Sterne's humor. Scherer finds in Sterne an essential disparity

> between the man himself and his destiny, between the whole of reality and the ideal which, rightly or wrongly, imposes itself on our minds as the law of things. The contrast is glaring on all sides. We hold ourselves formed for happiness and virtue, destined for everything that is true, noble, and sublime; and if we have the least touch of sincerity, we are obliged to recognise that we are weak, vacillating, limited, prosaic, fickle. . . . whence comes a great and all-pervading comedy, the human comedy, "Vanity Fair."

Sterne is not didactic, for he sees that "our absurdities are often the excuse or even the cloaks of virtue" and "our virtues have their absurd sides." As all great humorists, Sterne has the melancholy

[6]*Coleridge's Miscellaneous Criticism*, ed. Thomas Middleton Raysor (London: Constable, 1936), pp. 111-130. This scholarly reconstruction of Lecture IX from Coleridge's own notes is more reliable than the garbled version passed into the *Literary Remains* by Henry Nelson Coleridge (included in Raysor's edition as Appendix I, pp. 440-446).

which comes from seeing that the good and evil of man are inevitably connected:

> Nay, more, he takes pleasure in discovering everywhere vestiges of an original and indefeasible nobility. Still he knows at the same time that all of it has a seamy side, and he delights in turning that side out: in showing the tribe of narrownesses and absurdities that accompany virtue, the grotesque that pushes its way among things venerable and venerated. The views of our artist are tempered by a kind of melancholy: he laughs at humanity, but with no bitterness. The perception of the contrasts of human destiny by a man who does not sever himself from humanity, but who takes his own shortcomings and those of his dear fellow-creatures cheerfully—that is the essence of humor.[7]

The view of Sterne as a humorist in Jean Paul's sense is best represented in the twentieth century by Sir Herbert Read—although, in his two essays, Read mentions only Coleridge. Read's first comment was written for the *Times Literary Supplement* of May 26, 1927, and was republished in *The Sense of Glory*, 1929, and *Collected Essays in Literary Criticism*, 1938. The second was the introduction to his edition of the *Sentimental Journey*, Scholartis Press, 1929. Read goes beyond Jean Paul and Coleridge in explaining Sterne's humor as "classical."

> All real humorists are classicists, because it is the nature of a classicist to see things finite, and see things infinite, but not to confuse these two categories. The classicist, like the humorist, acknowledges the "hollowness and farce of the world, and its disproportion to the godlike within us"—and that is Coleridge's definition of humor.[8]

Unlike Coleridge, however, Read is prepared to defend Sterne's use of indecency. He especially takes to task George Saintsbury, who had said that Sterne could not laugh, but only snigger. "The snigger," answers Read, "is bitter and cynical, and Sterne is tender and generous." The sexuality and scatology are necessary to Sterne's humor:

> Life in his books is a tangled web of love and desire, but otherwise it would not be life, and if desire is treated, not as a dark

[7]*Essays on English Literature,* trans. George Saintsbury (New York: Charles Scribner's Sons, 1891), pp. 150-173.

[8]*Collected Essays in Literary Criticism* (London: Faber and Faber, 1938), p. 260.

and sinful horror to be supressed at any price, but as a natural
fact to be given its due place in the picture, we must not grumble
if this place is like the jester's at Court. ... humor is flat
and insipid unless it represents the contrast between the desires
of the flesh and the aspirations of the spirit.[9]

Finally, Read recasts the notion of humor into modern psychological
terms, concluding that Sterne was "the precursor of all psychological
fiction, which is as though we were to say: of all that is most significant in modern literature." [10]

Thus evolved a view of Sterne the humorist which accounted for
both his decency and indecency as parts of a moral comedy. The
next decade saw a resurgence of interest in the novelist. Lewis Perry
Curtis, the most exacting scholar to undertake a study of Sterne, pro-
duced his numerous articles and his revealing work on Sterne's
political career; Theodore Baird and others turned their attention toward Sterne's "philosophic" themes; and James Work's definitive edition of *Tristram Shandy* stimulated the public interest. It would
appear that Sterne, no longer regarded as either the high priest of the
cult of sensibility or the dirty prelate of filth, had at last won respectability as an artist.

But in 1940 came a change in critical approaches. That year Rufus
Putney published his article, "The Evolution of *A Sentimental
Journey*" (*PQ*, XIX, 349-369), answering a still-popular, though
somewhat old-fashioned interpretation of Sterne by Wilbur Cross,
Walter Sichel, Ernest Baker, and others. Sterne had written the
Journey, these writers thought, in a morbid emotional state brought
on by illness and a hopeless love for Eliza Draper. Putney, putting
to good use Curtis's scholarly edition of the letters, made a strong
case that Sterne was in relatively good health when writing the
Journey, and that he could hardly have been deeply in love with
Mrs. Draper. Without censuring Sterne, as had Thackeray, Putney
pointed out that Sterne lied to Eliza, addressed a love letter to her
identical to one he sent to another woman, and generally showed
himself an unreliable and inconstant lover. Putney revealed thus,
that Sterne approached the *Sentimental Journey* with the objectivity
of a humorist, not the subjectivity of a love-sick romantic. This
much of his argument was excellent, and a sufficient answer to the
flimsy theory he intended to refute.

[9]"Introduction," *A Sentimental Journey* (London: Scholartis Press,
1929), p. xxxv.
[10]*Collected Essays in Literary Criticism*, p. 264.

But Putney gave a twist to his interpretation which, I fear, has unfortunate implications, giving an air of respectability to the old charge that Sterne was "insincere." "Yorick's sentimental pose was adopted in response, not to Sterne's feelings but to popular demand for the pathos at which Sterne excelled." Putney traced out the gradual shift in *Tristram Shandy* toward pathetic scenes, arguing that these changes came in response to the demands of critics, especially those of Ralph Griffiths. At the last, Putney concluded that the *Journey* "was a hoax by which Sterne persuaded his contemporaries that the humor he wanted to write was the pathos they wished to read." In a later article, Putney extended his argument, but kept his thesis that the novel was a hoax: "To write and to laugh were still synonymous for him. He now solved his literary dilemma with a hoax by which he persuaded his contemporaries that the comedy he must write was the pathos they wished to read. He accomplished this by making Yorick weep in order that 'in the same tender moment' he himself might laugh." [11] Putney performed a service by pointing out the trickery whereby Sterne trips up any reader made awkward by his innocence or prudishness. On the other hand, Putney's view that Sterne purposely developed a sentimentality having little or no validity in man's moral nature, and that he did so in response to popular demand, has, I fear, insidious suggestions. If the joking Sterne who played fast and loose with sex and scatology is the true Sterne, if his benevolism and sensibility are for the most part sham, we are not apt seriously to concern ourselves with his work. In such a view Sterne is not the humorist of broad moral vision which Richter, Scherer, and Read have taken him to be.

In 1948 Ernest Nevin Dilworth published another version of the same general idea in his *Unsentimental Journey of Laurence Sterne.* Dilworth saw Sterne as a "thorough jester" who "differs from most of us in that he is so lightly constituted as to be able to make free with everything, and to find his chief pleasure in doing so" (p. 9). Dilworth took time for a careful and witty explication which has taught me, and I dare say many others, a great deal. Nevertheless, I cannot accept his opinion that Sterne's sentimentalism is a false-face made to appear serious and real only as a trick played upon the unsuspecting reader.

[11] "Laurence Sterne: Apostle of Laughter," in *The Age of Johnson: Essays Presented to Chauncey Brewster Tinker* (Yale University Press, 1949), pp. 159-170.

Sterne makes an odd sort of connoisseur of the feelings. He wrote the *Sentimental Journey* as a lark, but he threw the whole heart into his bubbling pot. A jester doesn't care so long as he amuses himself, but a declared satirist would do less damage. If Fielding had taken it into his head to do a *Sentimental Journey*, sentimentality would have been brilliantly mocked, but the heart would have been reset on a throne of tender truth. Not so in Sterne, where the merest good will is teased as if it were an extreme absurdity of the humanitarian vogue—and finally, like everything else, left in mid air by the juggler when a new toy of wit and whimsey sails into his sight. (p. 95)

Putney and Dilworth are right that Sterne's comic virtuosity has been read badly. But if some have blinded themselves to Sterne's lasciviousness, it is no answer to blind ourselves to his sympathy and tenderness. Putney and Dilworth regard Sterne as a literary mountebank, vending false sentimentality. It must be added that they defend very well Sterne's prerogative as a humorist to trick his readers. Nevertheless, the reader whose tears are beguiled by Yorick at the grave of the Monk or by the story of Le Fever must be Sterne's dupe. Since that interpretation makes me a dupe, I cannot accept it.

By revaluating the *Sentimental Journey*, I hope to fill a void left by Putney and Dilworth. To be sure, their sound scholarship and perceptive explications have nullified the damaging prudish view of Sterne epitomized by Thackeray and the misleading romantic view represented by Cross. Yet their ultimate interpretation of Sterne's sentimentalism as a hoax or burlesque has not won complete acceptance.[12] Puzzled by the matter, most recent scholars have avoided the *Journey* and confined their studies to the less sentimental *Tristram Shandy*. Few have come forth to defend Sterne as a great humorist. Ben Reid took the lead with his article, "The Sad Hilarity of Sterne" (*Virginia Quarterly Review*, XXXII), arguing that Sterne's humor belongs to "that great brand of comedy, like that of Shakespeare and Cervantes, which is rooted in the conviction of the radical imperfec-

---

[12]*E.g.*, see Alan McKillop, *Early Masters of English Fiction* (University of Kansas Press, 1956), p. 216: Putney's "demonstration that the *Journey* plays up the pathetic vein of *Shandy* is conclusive, but hardly justifies our pronouncing the *Journey* a 'hoax.' In another important article Putney treats the *Journey* as a subtle exposé of the errors of sentiment, as expounding a gospel of laughter rather than tears. But we are here dealing with a situation that cannot be resolved simply by setting laughter over against tears, or sincerity over against insincerity."

tion and imperfectibility of man's experience—what Unamuno calls 'the tragic sense of life.' " Reid sees Sterne as a moral writer, but in a much broader sense than didacticism, for Sterne writes about man as unsuccessful, about his visions and failures. And that is how he was regarded by Richter, Coleridge, Scherer, and Herbert Read. I should like to think that my own more detailed examination of the *Journey* and the sermons can help to keep alive the judgments of these men, that I can support their understanding of Sterne's pessimistically tender representation of comic man, trapped between his petty vileness and his noble ideals.

My method will be to compare the *Sentimental Journey* with Sterne's sermons; my purpose, to clarify that "radical imperfection" Sterne found in man's experience by measuring it against the perfection he could conceive aside from experience. I take seriously Sir Herbert Read's advice that "this paradox of a moral Sterne will be found more acceptable when the world begins to read that neglected half of Sterne's genius—his Sermons." It is unusual for a modern critic to think of Sterne's sermons as the production of genius. Yet, as Alan Howes' study reveals, they were once highly regarded. Sterne was not a very original moralist, but he was not thoughtlessly trite. No less an observer than Boswell thought of him as "the most taking composer of sermons that I have ever read." And Voltaire, in his article on conscience in the *Dictionnaire philosophique*, commented that the sermon "On the Abuses of Conscience Considered," as it appeared in *Tristram Shandy*, was "the best thing perhaps that was ever said upon this important subject" of a deceitful conscience.

Still, modern scholars have seldom searched the sermons for evidence of Sterne's beliefs. Since Dr. John Ferriar published his "Comments" in 1793, showing that Sterne plagiarized extensively in the sermons, critics have been shy of them. No doubt Sterne was a great plagiarist—by modern standards. That was the way his mind worked. But Hammond convinces one that Sterne's practices were hardly criminal by the standards of his profession at that time. And Sterne plagiarized from no one more extensively than from himself. The volume of borrowed passages is less than one might imagine— about 15,500 words; eleven per cent of the 140,000 words which comprise the published sermons.[13] If we are to understand him, we

[13]I arrived at my figure by, first, calculating the number of words in the passages Hammond thought were plagiarized, and which he collected together with the sources in his appendix. I then discounted this figure by

must accept this humorist for what he was. It is about as logical to close our eyes against his moral insights because his sermons are not entirely original as it would be to reject *Tristram Shandy* because Sterne borrowed many passages from Robert Burton's *Anatomy of Melancholy*.

Attempting to understand Sterne's moral, psychological, and religious views, we should accept as valid evidence even borrowed passages. Sterne plagiarized methodically, not aimlessly, taking from other writers what he himself believed. Hammond convincingly argues that Sterne kept a commonplace book of passages from published sermons which he thought might be useful. But he worked these into his own sermons with great dexterity. In "Temporal Advantages of Religion," he wove together verbatim transcripts from five disparate sources—Young, Blair, Clarke, Norris, and Tillotson. "And yet," comments Hammond, "these various fragments were joined together so skillfully that, when combined, they read as though one man had written them all, and at one time—truly an amazing performance." I would go beyond Hammond, however, to argue that so masterful a synthesis indicates that Sterne copied into his commonplace book only passages which expressed what he understood and believed. Had Sterne been no more than a charlatan trying to bluff his way through the duty of preaching, his patchwork would have appeared disjointed and illogical. His success in working these borrowings together could have been brought off only if he thoroughly understood them.

Nor can it be significant that Sterne composed all or most of the sermons a decade or more before *Trisram Shandy*. If he wrote them, as Hammond thinks, before 1751, he selected and edited twenty-seven of the extant forty-five during the period of the novels. True, the first two volumes (I-XV by modern numbering) were prepared for the press during Sterne's first visit to London when he was too busy being lionized to give them much attention. But the packet of homilies he brought from Sutton expressly to sell must have contained his favorites. The next two volumes (today numbered XVI-XXVII) Sterne edited at his leisure during the summer of 1765. If between 1751 and 1760 Sterne had altered considerably his moral and religious views, we might expect these twenty-seven sermons to be different in their doctrines from the untouched, posthumously-

---

one third to allow for Hammond's double entries and for the many "borrowings" he lists which are so very different in wording from the "sources" that I cannot agree with him.

published sermons (which are also, Hammond thinks, the earliest written). But I find no differences in doctrines or assumptions. The sermons Sterne saw through the press are much better in style, but the ideas are essentially the same throughout all of them. Furthermore, Sterne would surely have destroyed the yet un-published sermons had he not been willing to claim them as his thought, for during the period of the novels he was fully aware they would probably be published after his death. In 1761 he left a memorandum to his wife, "in case I should die abroad," which instructed her how to make the most of his effects. The first item is "my Sermons in a trunk at my friend Mr. Hall's, St. John Street.—2 Vols. to be picked out of them—NB. There are enough for 3 Vols" (*Letters*, p. 146).

Nothing in Sterne's history could justify a conclusion that either his religion or his sermons were insincere. It is quite true that his personal life was sometimes irregular.[14] However, he pursued his

[14]Because he was a clergyman, Sterne's moral faults have oddly affected his public image, though they are not very different from the faults of most people. On the one hand, a tendency to unscrupulousness in practical affairs has been largely ignored. Sterne's memory was not damaged by a none-too-clean political career as the tool of his bigoted uncle, Jaques Sterne, nor by his participation in two enclosures against the poor of common land. What shocked a puritanical public were his more personal weaknesses.

Sterne, it is frequently charged, mistreated his mother—"that dog Sterne," as Byron put it (borrowing words from Walpole), "who preferred whining over 'a dead ass to relieving a living mother.' " No doubt Sterne's self-defense (*Letters*, pp. 32-41) is biased, but there is little reason to doubt its essential accuracy. The gist of his crime is that he refused to invite his mother to move in with his bride. Mrs. Sterne had been living comfortably in Ireland when she heard exaggerated rumors of the wealth of her new daughter-in-law. She and Sterne's sister came immediately to England, demanding that Sterne set them up in finer style. Though financially pressed, Sterne gave them such cash as he had, pleading with them to return to Ireland. The situation was seized upon by his uncle, who was angry with Sterne for deserting his political campaigns; and the uncle did all he could to make matters worse, at one point lodging the mother "in that very place," as Sterne wrote, "where a hard report might do me (as a Clergyman) the most real disservice" (p. 33). Rumor has since identified the place as the common jail. The quarrel continued for several years, though it seems likely that Sterne and his mother were reconciled eventually (*Letters*, p. 61). These difficulties arose in the first place, I have no doubt, because Sterne did not want to inflict a grasping and unpleasant mother upon a wife who was emotionally unstable. His attitude shows in a letter of 1761, written after the mother had died but while the sister was still alive. Sterne, fearing for his own life, was instruct-

clerical duties, in the period before he took up novel writing, with a conscientiousness far beyond most of his contemporaries. Made a Canon of York Cathedral two years after he was ordained, for twenty years Sterne was a frequent and apparently very successful preacher at the great Minster. But most of his time was devoted to his rural parishes of Sutton-on-the-Forest and Stillington. For the seventeen years between 1742 and 1759, when he seriously took up writing, Sterne was a hard working parson, preaching twice every Sunday and conducting all parish business without the aid of a curate. The flock at Sutton alone consisted of two hundred and fifty potential communicants, and we can surmise that Sterne had considerable success among them from the fact that on one particular day, an Easter Sunday, half of these people actually took communion. This detail is known through Sterne's answers to a questionnaire sent out by Archbishop Herring in preparation for his Primary Visitation of 1743. Canon S. L. Ollard, who compared Sterne's answers to those of hundreds of other priests, found the reply to the ninth question particularly unusual,

> for it shows Sterne sufficiently zealous to hold a three-hours instruction or confirmation class in his vicarage on the six Sunday

---

ing his wife when he wrote, "If Lydia [their daughter] should die before you, leave my sister something worthy of yourself—in case you do not think it meet to purchase an annuity for your greater comfort: If you choose that—do it in God's name—" (p. 147). Yet, in the height of his anger, Sterne was one time decidedly cruel to his mother in casting a slur upon her birth when he must have known that she came from a genteel family (*Letters*, pp. 40-41; cf. p. 5, n. 2; p. 7, n. 13).

A second weakness which has damaged Sterne's reputation is the insatiable flirtatiousness which shows up so strongly during the last ten years of his unhappy marriage. His wife was not a winning person, but it is hard to forgive Sterne's open expression of a wish that she should die and free him. There are a few unconfirmed rumors that he was not always faithful to his marriage bed and patent evidence he did not want his wife with him during his last years. We know of many flirtations, and the stories of his intense courtships of Catherine Fourmantel and Eliza Draper are public records. Of recent years, however, this facet of Sterne's personality has not turned readers away from him. Loose sexual conduct among artists is now generally accepted as a fact which, however regrettable otherwise, does not detract from their artistic accomplishments.

Sterne was no paragon of virtue, but neither was he a blackguard. He was a doting father, faithful to his close friends, honest in his business dealings, and frank about his own shortcomings. Considering how neurotic and antagonistic were his mother, his uncle, and his wife, the wonder is that he did not become wholly bitter and cynical.

evenings in Lent (Evensong itself would, of course, have been said in the afternoon, as was the universal custom at that day). In all the hundreds of returns which Mr. Walker and I have examined this is unique and stands alone. It shows that in 1743, whatever was the case later, Sterne took his work as a parish priest very seriously.

Later Canon Ollard examined a second questionnaire sent out by Bishop Drummond in 1764, at the height of Sterne's literary career; and this showed "that Sterne's parishes were certainly not neglected, so far at any rate as services went."[15] When we imagine Sterne skipping about Europe in the heyday of his success while a paid curate was doing his parish work for him, we must remember that he skipped but weakly, for Sterne was then a dying man. While he had his strength, he was vigorous in the pursuit of priestly duties; and when he had it not, he saw to it that the duties were not neglected. Even in the later period, Sterne personally performed the functions of priest when called upon. A record has recently come to light of his winter at Toulouse in 1762-63. Archibald Bolling Shepperson has published hitherto unknown letters which Sterne wrote to the father and a friend of George Oswald, a young Englishman who died in Toulouse while under Sterne's care. The letters show Sterne exceptionally attentive and kind to this youth he had known for so short a while, making his inevitable passing as comfortable and peaceful as possible, and concerning himself to save the family as much pain as he could. These letters, comments Shepperson, reveal him "as a man of true sensibility, a sincere Christian who could act the rôle of good Samaritan with sympathy and understanding."[16]

Viewing the evidence as a whole, we can only conclude that Sterne was a sincere man of religion and an honest teacher of morality, that until his death he thought of his sermons as representing his beliefs. I shall, consequently, treat them as a record of his thinking.

[15] "Sterne as a Young Parish Priest," *TLS*, March 18, 1926, p. 217; "Sterne as Parish Priest," *TLS*, May 25, 1933, p. 364. Also see Ollard's self-correction of June 1, 1933, p. 380.

[16] "Yorick as Ministering Angel," *Virginia Quarterly Review*, XXX (1954), 54-66.

Chapter I

SENTIMENTAL COMMERCE

Laurence Sterne's *Sentimental Journey* is a work *sui generis*. As much a travel book as a novel, it is based upon Sterne's experiences on two trips to the continent. But unlike Fielding's *Voyage to Lisbon* or Johnson's *Journey to the Western Islands*, Sterne's travel book is highly fictionalized—an olio of incidents widely separated in time, stories Sterne picked up from others, and fictions of his own imagination. A number of the characters appearing in the book were historic personages Sterne had known. Others have not been identified, and are probably the products of Sterne's art. Sterne avoided descriptions of buildings and cities in the manner of commonplace travel books. He had satirized such writing in the seventh volume of *Tristram Shandy*. In the *Journey* his ride through Versailles itself could produce "nothing which I look for in traveling," a mere "blank" to be filled with a sentimental story. He made his narrator an Anglican priest, like himself, and gave him his own physical appearance and infirmities. He gave to this semifictional narrator-protagonist the name Yorick, under which Sterne had already published his sermons and drawn an idealized self-portrait in *Tristram Shandy*. Sterne then allowed Yorick from time to time to slip into a second-person address to his own current inamorata, Eliza. "I am well aware," announces Yorick, "both my travels and observations will be altogether of a different cast from any of my forerunners."

Yorick, who is interested exclusively in the human contacts made by a traveler, commits himself early to a particular moral point of view. He undertakes to give an answer to the splenetic opinions of Tobias Smollett, in *Travels through France and Italy*, and Samuel Sharp, in *Letters from Italy* (both 1766). These two physicians-turned-writers Sterne introduced into his pages as Smelfungus and Mundungus.

> Mundungus, with an immense fortune, made the whole tour; going on from Rome to Naples—from Naples to Venice—from Venice to Vienna—to Dresden, to Berlin, without one generous

connection or pleasurable anecdote to tell of; but he had traveled straight on looking neither to his right hand or his left, lest Love or Pity should seduce him out of his road. (pp. 51-52)

Still sharper stings are given to Smollett:

> The learned Smelfungus traveled from Boulogne to Paris— from Paris to Rome—and so on—but he set out with the spleen and jaundice, and every object he passed by was discolored or distorted—He wrote an account of them, but 'twas nothing but the account of his miserable feelings.
>
> . . . I popped upon Smelfungus again at Turin, in his return home; and a sad tale of sorrowful adventures he had to tell, "wherein he spoke of moving accidents by flood and field, and of the cannibals which each other eat: the Anthropophagi"—he had been flayed alive, and bedeviled, and used worse than St. Bartholomew, at every stage he had come at—
>
> —I'll tell it, cried Smelfungus, to the world. You had better tell it, said I, to your physician. (pp. 50-51)

Although one admires Smollett's frankness, it must be admitted that he gives the impression of being a thorough curmudgeon. While not excluding Englishmen from his sarcasm, he could not stand foreign manners. Every post seems painful, and he never evidences warmth or sympathy for those he meets. Politeness he defines in his book as "the art of making one's self agreeable," an art requiring "a sense of decorum, and a delicacy of sentiment." But, he goes on, "these are qualities, of which (as far as I have been able to observe) a Frenchman has no idea; therefore he never can be deemed polite, except by those persons among whom they are as little understood." The suavity of the French gentleman evokes his special scorn:

> This attendance is not the effect of attachment, or regard, but of sheer vanity, that he may afterwards boast of his charity and humane dispositions: though, of all the people I have ever known, I think the French are the least capable of feeling for the distresses of their fellow creatures. Their hearts are not susceptible of deep impressions; and, such is their levity, that the imagination has not time to brood long over any disagreeable idea, or sensation.[1]

[1]*Travels through France and Italy*, intro. Thomas Seccombe (Oxford University Press, 1919), pp. 60-61. Gardner D. Stout, in the notes to his yet unpublished edition of the *Journey*, traces in detail Sterne's spoof

Sterne seems to announce early that to these opinions his *Sentimental Journey* will be an "answer." Throughout the book he concentrates upon the politeness, the humanity, the sensibility of the French people. Had he lived to complete the volumes on Italy, no doubt the Italians would have been approached in the same frame of mind. Yorick, a "sentimental traveler," searches for moral sentiments.[2] If Mundungus would look "neither to his right hand or his left, lest Love or Pity should seduce him out of his road," Yorick, searching all about for Love and Pity, would not worry if he got nowhere.

The reader of the *Sentimental Journey* will err, however, if he takes too seriously Yorick's passion for "sentimental commerce." Sterne's contrasting the moral sensibility of his narrator to the hard, critical attitudes of Smollett and Sharp constitutes only a device for launching a work, the major effect of which remains outside mawkish sentimentality. In fact, the comedy of Sterne's book arises from the obsessive zeal with which Yorick seeks out Love and Pity.

The opening scenes demonstrate the point. Responding to a whim, Yorick packs a single portmanteau, takes the packet to Calais, and "by three I had got sat down to my dinner upon a fricaseed chicken . . . incontestibly in France." The French, he has decided previously, are "a people so civilized and courteous, and so renowned for sentiment and fine feeling" (p. 2). His prejudiced view is somewhat disordered, however, by a chance thought: what is he to make of the cruel French law, the *Droits d'aubaine*, which allows the crown to seize all the possessions of a foreigner dying on French soil? A good meal and a bottle of wine with which to drink the health of the French king puts Yorick back into a benevolent frame of mind and convinces him that he feels for the monarch "no spleen, but on the contrary, high honor for the humanity of his temper." Elated by

---

of Smollett, Sharp, and other travelers. See his Stanford dissertation, *A Sentimental Journey through France and Italy by Mr. Yorick.*

[2]Sterne's title must have suggested his focus upon moral problems. The word *sentimental* which all philologists agree Sterne popularized (although they still disagree about whether he invented it), is created out of the word *sentiment,* which meant roughly "a moral evaluation, an attitude of approval or disapproval from a moral point of view." See Erik Erämetsä, *Study of the Word 'Sentimental'* (Helsinki, 1951), p. 23. Shaftesbury, Hutcheson, Hume, and Adam Smith made such widespread use of the word *sentiment* in their philosophical ethics that today they are sometimes designated as the "sentimental school." It may be that Sterne impelled the word toward its modern pejorative, as Erämetsä believes, but at the time of the appearance of the *Journey,* the word *sentimental* very likely was taken to mean "moral."

the good wine and easy charity—"no—said I—the Bourbon is by
no means a cruel race: they may be misled like other people"—
he lightly kicks aside the portmanteau which had called to mind
the *Droits d'aubaine*. Yorick is in a mood to think the entire world
made up of "kind-hearted brethren," albeit many "fall out so cruelly"
through a love of material goods. Obviously, Yorick is infatuated
with the idea of courtesy and kindness. He has as yet found no
goodness in the French people, whom he has hardly seen, nor in
their king, whom he will never see, nor in himself. Yorick sets out
on his travels possessed of that not-uncommon vanity by which, seeing benevolence indiscriminately in all humanity, he can assume it
in himself.

His self-flattery and self-deception are at once contrasted to the
frankness and humility of the Monk. The more to enjoy his goodness of heart, Yorick stands up in the café and pulls out his purse:
"When man is at peace with man, how much lighter than a feather
is the heaviest of metals in his hand! He pulls out his purse, and
holding it airily and uncompressed, looks round him, as if he sought
for an object to share it with" (pp. 3-4). While he stands thus tipsily,
feeling the dilation of every vessel of his frame, feeling the "arteries
beat all cheerily," beginning even to identify himself with that same
humane Bourbon—"Now, was I a king of France"—purse in hand
and looking for an object with which to share it, the eleemosynary
monk enters. Yorick's benevolence collapses: "The moment I cast
my eyes upon him, I was predetermined not to give him a single
sou." True, as a Protestant clerygman he has some doctrinal differences with the Roman mendicant orders; yet Yorick goes beyond
such disagreements and is positively rude as well as ungenerous. All
his easy virtue—easy so long as no charitable action is required—
can give no more than unkind words to a modest, courteous, re-
spectable man who asks an alms for the love of God.

The acute reader realizes that within a few pages Sterne has offered an unexpected answer to Smollett. Whereas Smollett, in his
travel book, appears pompous, grumpy, and self-centered, Yorick
appears frivolous, credulous, and self-centered. Far from displaying
human benevolence, Sterne in this opening questions its reality.

Yet Sterne knows that sympathy and good-will are realities which,
if not easily found, are still to be discovered. They are taught Yorick
by the Monk in their second meeting. But before this second en-
counter Yorick makes the acquaintance of a charming Fleming,
"Madame de L***," and his interest in her sets the stage for the

moral lesson. The lady apparently has had a previous acquaintance with the Monk, and when Yorick sees the two chatting, he decides the Franciscan must be telling her about his own rude conduct (p. 26). He plots, therefore, "to undo the ill impressions" (p. 31). The Monk approaches the lady and Yorick as they are talking in the courtyard. Politely he holds out his snuff-box to Yorick. Yorick in turn holds out his own, claiming hypocritically that it is "the peace-offering of a man who once used you unkindly, but not from the heart" (p. 32). The stratagem only uncovers the falsity of his solicitude: "The poor Monk blushed as red as scarlet. *Mon Dieu!* said he, pressing his hands together—you never used me unkindly. —I should think, said the lady, he is not likely." Then, in mock secrecy, Sterne offers the key to the scene: "I blushed in my turn; but from what movements, I leave to the few who feel to analyze." The reader who wants to savor Sterne's humor always stops to analyze such comments. Yorick blushes, it seems to me, because the brief interpolation of the lady had suddenly revealed to him how impossible it was that the Monk had said anything to her about his rudeness. The "movements" which brought about the blush are chagrin at having misjudged, shame for having thought ill of a genuinely kind man who held no grudge and sought no revenge. Distrust shattered, the courtship temporarily forgotten, the three share a short moment of perfect good will.

> We remained silent, without any sensation of that foolish pain which takes place, when in such a circle you look for ten minutes in one another's faces without saying a word. Whilst this lasted, the Monk rubbed his horn box upon the sleeve of his tunic; and as soon as it had acquired a little air of brightness by the friction—he made a low bow, and said, 'twas too late to say whether it was the weakness or the goodness of our tempers which had involved us in this contest—but be it as it would—he begged we might exchange boxes—In saying this, he presented his to me with one hand, as he took mine from me in the other; and having kissed it—with a stream of good-nature in his eyes he put it into his bosom—and took his leave. (pp. 33-34)

This famous scene expresses, I believe, Sterne's ideal of amity. It was taken very seriously in the eighteenth century. In Germany groups of Sterne votaries used to exchange snuff-boxes to symbolize their vows of forgiveness and pity. Today, conditioned by Freudianism and *Nightmare Alley*, we are not so trustful of it. I would argue, nevertheless, that the scenes with the Monk are about the "weakness or goodness of our tempers," and as a whole they amount to Yorick's first lesson in benevolence. Only that interpretation can make plausible the otherwise puzzling incident which immediately follows the snuff-box scene, although it jumps ahead in time. When he later heard of the Monk's death, Yorick tells us, he went to visit the grave: "upon pulling out his little horn box, as I sat by his grave, and plucking up a nettle or two at the head of it, which had no business to grow there, they all struck together so forcibly upon my affections, that I burst into a flood of tears" (pp. 34-35). The added plea is especially difficult for a twentieth-century reader to accept—"but I am as weak as a woman; and I beg the world not to smile, but pity me." Yorick's weakness is not the giving way to tears, but his moral weakness in the entire experience. His plea for pity is made in character—the frail moral character he is to uncover as the *Sentimental Journey* moves along. His warning not to laugh tips us off that he sees himself as a fool.

If we read the *Journey* as a modern novel instead of a moral tract, if we are willing to seek out its implied ideal without expecting the protagonist to arrive at perfection, if we give ourselves to the human drama of clashing weaknesses and virtues, we shall discover in it, not the "course of morality" which Thomas Jefferson found in the book, but the moral experience found by Jean Paul. Nor should we go to an extreme, with Rufus Putney and Ernest Nevin Dilworth, to read the *Journey* as a burlesque of sentimental fiction. The *Sentimental Journey* is very much a moral book, as it is also a comedy. The two categories do not exclude each other.

Sterne's book takes account of a common human experience, each man's hunger for sympathy and exchanges of good-will which is frustrated by his own egocentricity. The groundwork for this comedy of moral sentiments rests in the simple psychological and moral assumptions Sterne reveals in his sermons. Sterne there holds that man comes into the world accoutered with natural benevolence; but he also believes man has a host of selfish passions which are equally natural. If the first meeting with the Monk ends by exposing Yorick's self-love, that kind man eventually shows Yorick a tolerance and love which Sterne considers a substantial part of human conduct.

In the sermons, Sterne assumes that man is psychologically motivated by a set of natural instincts and appetites, some of which prompt man toward morally admirable actions, some of which drive him toward conduct morally reprehensible. Because he believes these impulses direct man toward specific objects, he is what we might call an "instinct psychologist." But whatever the term, Sterne's position can be sharply distinguished from two other schools of thought. He is not an "egoist"; that is, he does not think all motivating forces are but manifestations of a single general principle of self-love. And he is not an "association psychologist," such as Hartley, who believes that people slowly evolve their drives and desires through experience and training.[3]

"The Vindication of Human Nature," Sterne's seventh sermon, attacks the self-love school of moralists by arguing for the naturalness of benevolent instincts. One guesses the sermon is aimed at Mandeville, but Sterne might have had in mind Archibald Campbell, Thomas Rutherforth, or any number of minor writers. Without naming an antagonist, Sterne sets out to defeat the self-love philosophers who maintain "the truest definition that can be given" of man, "is this, that he is a selfish animal" (Vol. I, p. 112).

Sterne's method in the "Vindication" is to describe commonplace evidences of man's disinterested conduct. He first depicts a typical youth: "how warmly, how heartily he enters into friendships,—how disinterested, and unsuspicious in the choice of them,—how generous and open in his professions!—how sincere and honest in making them good" (Vol. I, p. 118). For Sterne, youth is not selfish; the only criticism the young deserve is that of being foolishly generous. In

[3]Bishop Joseph Butler, a leading expositor of the ancient doctrine I have called "instinct psychology," distinguishes between particular benevolent instincts and a more general altruistic principle, between particular impulses of self-love and a general selfish principle. See especially Sermons XI and XII in *Works*, Vol. II, ed. W. E. Gladstone (Oxford: Clarendon, 1896). For a discussion of Sterne's differences with the associationists, see my study, "The Lockean Psychology of *Tristram Shandy*," *ELH*, XXII (1955), 125-135. I there maintain that the much-discussed associationism of *Tristram Shandy* is not radical to the organization of that book, but a peripheral embellishment. Although by Sterne's time associationism was the most advanced of all psychological theories, Sterne was interested only in Locke's older, cruder theory for its comic possibilities. The sermons bear out this conclusion, for in them Sterne never mentions the doctrine of association. He does, however, consistently assume the much older notion of instincts or drives or passions. And he is not alone, for his assumption is shared by such divers thinkers as Bishop Butler; Samuel Clarke, "The Great Duty of Universal Love and Charity," *Works* (London, 1738), Vol. II, 385-393; and, curiously, the moral work of David Hume, whose associationism in other contexts is well-known—*Enquiry Concerning the Principles of Morals*, Appendix II, in *Enquiries*, ed. L. A. Selby-Bigge (Oxford: Clarendon, 1902), especially pp. 301-302.

maturity too, man displays "the same benevolence of heart altered only in its course," so that he now gives himself to his family, "spending many weary days, and sleepless nights—utterly forgetful of himself" (Vol. I, pp. 119-120). Nor is the case altered when he acts, not as a father of a family, but as a man without ties: "He cannot stop his ears against the cries of the unfortunate.—The sad story of the fatherless and him that has no helper *must* be heard . . . and a thousand other untold cases of distress to which the life of man is subject, find a way to his heart, let interest guide the passage as it will" (Vol. I, pp. 121-122). One of the most moving of Sterne's sermons, the "Vindication" is a convincing argument, at a common sense level, for the naturalness of benevolent impulses.

Sermon III, "Philanthropy Recommended," takes Sterne's concept a step further. "There is something in our nature," Sterne explains, "which engages us to take part in every accident to which man is subject." But when we view another in a truly calamitous situation, we discover that our interest does not arise from imagining ourselves in the position of the unfortunate. We may make the troubles "our own," but we do so "from a certain generosity and tenderness of nature which disposes us for compassion, abstracted from all considerations of self" (Vol. I, pp. 38-39). This benevolence is instinctive and spontaneous: "the impulse to pity is so sudden that, like instruments of music which obey the touch—the objects which are fitted to excite such impressions work so instantaneous an effect, that you would think the will was scarce concerned" (Vol. I, p. 45).

This was published eight years before the *Sentimental Journey*; probably it was written eighteen years before. I do not think, with Dilworth, that Sterne was a jester "who, finding lachrymosity lying in his way, took it for a considerable part of his subject matter." For Sterne the priest, benevolence was a facet of human nature which, when properly nurtured, played a major role in the character of goodness. If his novels turn upon man's difficulty in exposing this side of his nature, Sterne did not view benevolence as a hollow, faddish notion. There is no mockery in his treatment of Trim, manfully protecting Susannah after she had allowed the window sash to circumcise small Hero. There is no satire in the old French officer's concern for Yorick and the mistreated dwarf at the Opéra Comique. Who can find fault with Uncle Toby's kindness to Le Fever?[4] Even the description of Uncle Toby in the last volume of

⁴Dilworth has trouble, it seems to me, explaining away the story of Le Fever. Since in that tale Uncle Toby never wavers in his benevolence,

Tristram Shandy reads like a passage from one of Sterne's sermons. Nature, says Tristram, had formed Uncle Toby

> of the best and kindliest clay—had tempered it with her own milk, and breathed into it the sweetest spirit—she had made him all gentle, generous and humane—she had filled his heart with trust and confidence, and disposed every passage which led to it, for the communication of the tenderest offices. (p. 626)

But hold on, Dilworth would be likely to say; finish the quotation. After all, Sterne is explaining why Uncle Toby would make a good husband. Sterne goes on to point out that Nature

> had moreover considered the other causes for which matrimony was ordained—

---

since at this point sex does not intrude, Dilworth must explain the joke by the style alone. For instance, he discusses the description of the death itself, which I reproduce here: "Nature instantly ebbed again,—— the film returned to its place,——the pulse fluttered——stopped——went on ——throbbed——stopped again——moved——stopped——" (p. 426). About these lines Dilworth exclaims, "That was more like it. There's the Shandean vein. One could continue for a whole page of stops and starts, but not this time. 'Shall I go on?' he asks. And in one word, the Comic Spirit, leaping from his pen, says '——No' " —*The Unsentimental Journey of Laurence Sterne* (New York: King's Crown, 1948), pp. 25-26. One cannot *answer* Dilworth's reading. There is no way of proving with certainty the meaning of Sterne's question and answer, "Shall I go on?—— No." Dilworth takes the line to mean, *Shall I go on with the joke?* But if one is moved by the story of Le Fever, he will read the line as, *Shall I go on with the pain of this scene?* Sterne himself left two indications that he thought he had written a lovely story. When he dedicated Volumes V and VI of *Tristram Shandy* to Lord Spencer, he begged leave to inscribe the Le Fever story to Lady Spencer, "for which I have no other motive, which my heart has informed me of, but that the story is a humane one" (probably the very line Sterne read aloud to Dr. Johnson, which caused Johnson to pronounce, "That is not English, Sir!"—Cross, p. 284). It does not seem likely Sterne would have risked this inscription to the lady of his patron had he expected his most perceptive readers to discover that the story was a joke or a hoax. Sterne's attitude is probably expressed in a letter to a Lady D——: " 'Le Fever's story has beguiled your ladyship of your tears,' and the thought of the accusing spirit flying up to heaven's chancery with the oath, you are kind enough to say is sublime—my friend Mr. Garrick, thinks so too, and I am most vain of his approbation ——your ladyship's opinion adds not a little to my vanity" (*Letters,* p. 150).

And accordingly   *   *   *   *   *
*   *   *   *   *   *   *   *
*   *   *   *   *   *   *   *

Dilworth's opinion would be, I am sure, that the dirtiness of those
little stars invalidates the description of Uncle Toby's goodness.
Edmond Scherer and Herbert Read would probably say, to the
contrary, that here we have the comic vision of concomitant idealism
and carnality.

A study of the sermons Sterne published tends to strengthen the
interpretation represented by Scherer and Read, rather than that
of Dilworth. Sterne took seriously a perfectly orthodox doctrine of
man's radical sinfulness. Self-love is for him as real as benevolence.
The divine purpose in sympathetic affections, Sterne explains, is to
act as "a check upon too great a propensity toward self-love"
(Vol. I, p. 73). Throughout the sermons Sterne sets over against
natural benevolence the equally natural, but opposing vices—"the
worst of human passions,—pride . . . hypocrisy, self-love, covetousness, extortion, cruelty and revenge" (Vol. I, p. 99). The chief purpose of religion is to teach us how we can subdue "all those unfriendly
dispositions in our nature" (Vol. II, p. 313), for without the aid of
God, the "stream of our affections and appetites but too naturally
carries us the other way" (Vol. II, p. 277). The words spoken by
Christ, "I come not to send peace on earth, but a sword," symbolize
for Sterne "the inward contests and opposition which Christianity
would occasion in the heart of man,—from its oppositions to the
violent passions of our nature,—which would engage us in perpetual
warfare. . . . it was dividing a man against himself;—setting up an
opposition to an interest long established,—strong by nature . . ."
(Vol. II, p. 318). Sometimes these tendencies toward sin are "fretful passions" (Vol. II, p. 314). More often they are described as
an enemy army—the "violent enemies" of man who have formed
a strong "interest" and "rebelled" against virtue (Vol. I, pp. 306-
307). Sterne's favorite metaphor, however, is a traditional one—the
storm: those "turbulent and haughty passions which disturb our
quiet" (Vol. II, p. 60), the "stormy wind and tempest, which He
has planted in our hearts" (Vol. II, p. 36), the "fretful storm of passions, which hurry men on to acts of revenge" (Vol. I, p. 206).
Nature has endowed man with native tendencies toward evil as well
as propensities for good.

True, the more orthodox view of man's sinfulness is not so con-

spicuous in the sermons as Sterne's thesis about benevolence. Sterne
wanted to prove what most of his parishioners did not believe—
that charity and friendship are "planted in our hearts" (Vol. II,
pp. 36-37; *cf.* Vol. I, pp. 116, 290). It is a favorite theme that "the
general propensity to pity the unfortunate, we express . . . by the
word *humanity*, as if it was inseparable from our nature" (Vol. I,
pp. 48-49).[5] Since everyone knew about sin, Sterne was less anxious
to describe the anatomy of evil. Passions such as self-preservation
(Vol. I, pp. 323-324) and ambition (Vol. I, p. 220) he gave but
summary treatment.[6] Nevertheless, a perusal of the sermons leaves
no doubt that benevolence and self-love are both deeply rooted in
man's emotional constitution.[7] This should be a sufficient answer to

[5]Hammond, p. 161, thinks this is borrowed from Tillotson's ninth sermon. Sterne's wording, however, does not closely resemble that of
Tillotson.

[6]The sexual passions, which figure so largely in the novels, are not described in the sermons. Chastity Sterne mentioned in passing as a duty
(Vol. I, p. 307; Vol. II, p. 341), but apparently he thought the description of sexual desire no fit subject for the pulpit. Trim's confession of his feelings for the fair Beguine in *Tristram Shandy* (pp. 570-575)
leaves no doubt, however, that the sex drive belongs in a class with the
other instinctive appetites.

[7]I may distort slightly Sterne's terminology by speaking of self-love
and benevolence as opposing classes of affections in his "system," but
not, I think, his general meaning. Sterne uses the word *benevolence* in the
typical way of his time, which had been popularized by Hutcheson: the
word means any charitable, loving, compassionate affection, that is,
the *emotional impulse* (in a variety of forms) to make another happy.
As the etymological meaning ("well-wishing") suggests, the word can
and has had very broad denotations. It had been an omnibus term for
Bishop Richard Cumberland, the first moral philosopher to make much
use of it. According to Hutcheson, Cumberland meant by the word any
"internal spring of virtue"—*Inquiry into the Original of our Ideas of
Beauty and Virtue* (London, 1738), p. 177. Hutcheson, however, narrowed the meaning to affections—as distinct from reason—but any of a
variety of emotions which require the welfare of another. About this time,
most moralists began to use the word *self-love* as a counterpart to benevolence in the Hutchesonian sense: self-love designates any affection
which demands the welfare of the agent himself. This is the meaning I
have in mind when I use the term. But actually, Sterne uses the word in
a somewhat narrow and unusual way. He may speak of self-love as a
specific passion classed with other instincts having particular objects. (Vol.
I, p. 183); or he may mean the tendency of man to flatter himself and
deceive himself (Vol. I, p. 229; Vol. II, pp. 61, 214); and sometimes he
seems to give it a meaning approximating what we would call the "pleasure
principle" (Vol. II, p. 49).

all who would claim Sterne's benevolism was affected or his indecency fortuitous.

Left to nature alone, man, as Sterne understood him, would be impelled first one way and then another. At one moment he might be selfish and mean, at the next generous and kind. Indeed, Sterne's most simple form of sentimental comedy consists of a mere presentation of this natural capriciousness. When Yorick in the *Sentimental Journey* prepares to leave the inn at Montreuil, he gets set to satisfy the beggars waiting outside. Since this is to be his first public act of charity in France, he self-consciously and smugly goes about being a *good* man. He steps forth to give away generously all of eight *sous*, only to discover sixteen beggars. Instead of reaching for more money, Yorick gives in to the flattery of the ragged crowd and begins to buy their compliments.

> *Mon cher et très chéritable Monsieur*—There's no opposing this, said I.
> *My Lord Anglois*—the very sound was worth the money—so I gave *my last sou for it*.

But suddenly he sees the *pauvre honteux*, the shamefaced beggar, standing outside the circle, wiping a tear from a face that had seen better days:

> Good God! said I—and I have not one single *sou* left to give him—But you have a thousand! cried all the powers of nature, stirring within me—so I gave him—no matter what—I am ashamed to say *how much*, now—and was ashamed to think, how little, then. (pp. 67-68)

Yorick has his good points and his bad. When we walk all around him, to see him whole, he makes us laugh.

So too in *Tristram Shandy*. In his genial way, for Sterne is never bitter, he describes Walter Shandy as "frank and generous in his nature," but with a "little soreness of temper." Certain "little ebullitions of this subacid humor toward others" urges Walter to torment his brother Toby in his most "tender" part—his hobby. But with comic suddenness, Walter will drop his torture to become once more a doting brother (pp. 114-115, 211-212).

Yorick's egoistic proclivities are less acid than those of Walter Shandy, as his craving for feelings of benevolence and sympathy is more intense. His major adventures on the road to Paris and his experiences the first evening in that city, which make up the first volume of the *Journey*, all expose the foolishness of a seeker after benevolence who is blinded by his own self-concerns.

At Montreuil he hires a servant, La Fleur, in a sentimental manner.

> I am apt to be taken with all kinds of people at first sight; but never more so, than when a poor devil comes to offer his services to so poor a devil as myself; and as I know this weakness, I always suffer my judgment to draw back something on that very account—and this more or less, according to the mood I am in, and the case—and I may add the gender too, of the person I am to govern. (p. 56)

La Fleur is not of the proper gender, but the case is one of necessity, and the mood is perfect. So "the genuine look and air of the fellow determined the matter at once in his favor," and the next morning they leave Montreuil, La Fleur cantering away before, "as happy and as perpendicular as a prince."

Before they have gone a league, they come upon the carcass of a dead ass.

> A dead ass . . . put a sudden stop to La Fleur's career—his bidet would not pass by it—a contention arose betwixt them, and the poor fellow was kicked out of his jack-boots the very first kick.

> La Fleur bore his fall like a French Christian, saying neither more nor less upon it, than, *Diable!* so presently got up and came to the charge again astride his bidet, beating him up to it as he would have beat his drum.

> The bidet flew from one side of the road to the other, then back again—then this way—then that way, and in short every way but by the dead ass.—La Fleur insisted upon the thing—and the bidet threw him. (pp. 69-70)

I have quoted the scene in full because I want to emphasize that the focus of attention is not upon the dead animal, as most critics would have it, but upon the live one. And it is a cruel picture Sterne paints of a terrified horse being mistreated by a hot-headed ex-drummer. Eventually, at the suggestion of Yorick, La Fleur gives the horse "a good sound lash" and sends her flying home again.

If there is an object in the *Sentimental Journey* which deserves pity, it is this frightened beast. Yorick has none for it. Instead he chooses to discourse upon the three degrees of the French curse, crying out in ironic mock sympathy about the superlative curse, "But here my heart is wrung with pity and fellow-feeling, when I reflect what miseries must have been their lot, and how bitterly so refined a people must have smarted, to have forced them upon the use of it." The hyperbole is light; the serious consideration is that Yorick does not even notice how unfeeling has been his cheerful "complexional philosopher" companion. Yorick is careless of the pitiable, but greedy for pathos.

He has every opportunity to satisfy his hunger at the next stage, where he discovers the old German peasant who had owned the dead animal. "And this, said he, putting the remains of a crust into his wallet—and this, should have been thy portion, said he, hadst thou been alive to have shared it with me.—I thought by the accent, it had been an apostrophe to his child; but 'twas to his ass." As the villagers gather about him, the old man tells the story of how he had traveled to Spain to give thanks to St. Iago for sparing one of his sons from death by small-pox. He tells how he loved the beast, his only friend and companion on his journey. "Shame on the world!" says Yorick to himself. "Did we love each other as this poor soul but loved his ass—'twould be something" (p. 75). Yorick's assumption that Christian love among men is of a kind with the dotage of an old man for an animal is patently silly. Following so soon after La Feur's unnoticed cruelty to the horse, the remark shows clearly how blind is Yorick to the realities of moral sentiment.

The chapter which immediately follows intensifies the contrast between Yorick's infatuation with the idea of pity and the cruel treatment of animals. Yorick, wanting to muse upon the sentimental scene of the old man's grief, asks the postillion to move at a slow pace. The postillion, however, gives "an unfeeling lash to each of his beasts, and set off clattering like a thousand devils (p. 76). After Yorick has been thoroughly—shaken into a "foolish passion," the man slows down to a walk that Yorick "may enjoy the sweets of it." Yorick's exasperated utterance speaks more eloquently for his entire sentimental travel than he himself realizes—"The deuce go, said I, with it all! Here am I sitting as candidly disposed to make the best of the worst, as ever wight was, and all runs counter" (p. 77).

The events at Amiens center upon the arrival there of Madame de L***, the lovely lady Yorick had met at Calais, and for whom he has a sentimental attachment. While raising no serious problems for the reader, the interlude serves to remind him of a theme which is, we shall later see, central to the comedy—the association of moral sentiments with sexual desire. While Yorick frets about dividing his loyalties between this fascinating widow and the Eliza he had left in England, La Fleur embroils him in the necessity of writing a *billet-doux*. Yorick vamps up a note from one provided by La Fleur as a model—a letter from a drummer to a corporal's wife, which affirms that "l'amour n'est *rien* sans sentiment. Et le sentiment est encore *moins* sans amour" (p.86).

The sexual overtones are unmistakable in the apostrophe to courtesy with which Yorick opens the account of his first sentimental adventure in the city of Paris:

> Hail, ye small sweet courtesies of life, for smooth do ye make the road of it! Like grace and beauty which beget inclinations to love at first sight; 'tis ye who open this door and let the stranger in. (p. 93)

Yorick, in need of directions to the Opéra Comique, had cast an eye into many shops "in search of a face not likely to be disordered" by an inquiry; the one he entered was the first shop cared for by a beautiful woman. Yet Yorick informs us he is investigating only courtesy:

> I will not suppose it was the woman's beauty, notwithstanding she was the handsomest *grisette*, I think, I ever saw, which had much to do with the sense I had of her courtesy; only I remember, when I told her how much I was obliged to her, that I looked very full in her eyes,—and that I repeated my thanks as often as she had done her instructions. (pp. 94-95)[8]

Yorick, thoroughly rattled, cannot remember her instructions. She repeats them three times, "and if *tones and manners* have a meaning, which certainly they have, unless to hearts which shut them out—she seemed really interested, that I should not lose myself." But Yorick still cannot remember—"Is it possible! said she, half laughing.—'Tis very possible, replied I, when a man is thinking more of a woman, than of her good advice. As this was real truth— she took it, as every woman takes a matter of right, with a slight courtesy.—*Attendez!* said she, laying her hand upon my arm . . .";

[8] I have changed Sterne's spelling of *grisset*, to the more common *grisette*. This word, no longer in widespread use, meant a young woman of the *peuple*, typically dressed in grey, and by connotation, typically of easy virtue.

and she calls to a boy at the back of the shop to guide Yorick. While
waiting for the boy, Yorick, in one of the most comical sentimental
scenes in fiction, continues his moral investigation by feeling her
pulse to determine whether the "temperature" of her heart "descends
to the extremes." Out of Yorick's thoughts during the counting and
the small events in the shop, Sterne skillfully compounds a psychological study of the good and evil in his protagonist. Sexual excite-
ment of which Yorick is hardly aware reveals itself in Yorick's
speculations about morality in the form which the woman seems to
epitomize—courtesy. A man enters the room: " 'Twas nobody but
her husband, she said—So I began a fresh score—Monsieur is so
good, quoth she, as he passed by us, as to give himself the
trouble of feeling my pulse—The husband took off his hat, and
making me a bow, said, I did him too much honor—and having
said that, he put on his hat and walked out" (p. 98). This sets
off a chain of reflections upon the French shopkeeper, a "rough
son of Nature," and his polished wife, whom Yorick contrasts to the
London shop merchant and his wife who "seem to be one bone
and one flesh: in the several endowments of mind and body, sometimes the one, sometimes the other has it, so as in general to be upon
a par, and to tally with each other as nearly as man and wife need
to do" (pp. 98-99). Sterne climaxes this sexual-ethical inquiry
with a masterful visual touch symbolic of Sterne's vision of man's
ambivalence: "And how does it beat, Monsieur? said she.—With
all the benignity, said I, looking quietly in her eyes, that I expected."

But the incident ends rather sadly in a discovery that the woman's
courtesy is as shallow as Yorick's investigation. Prompted, apparently,
by feelings of guilt, Yorick is anxious to buy a pair of gloves. They
can find none which fit. The *grisette*, seemingly for mercenary reasons, will sell him an outsized pair. They loll indecisively upon the
narrow counter until the sentimental scene flares, for an instant, into
one of distrust and contention.

> The beautiful *grisette*, looked sometimes at the gloves, then
> side-ways to the window, then at the gloves—and then at me.
> I was not disposed to break silence—I followed her example:
> so I looked at the gloves, then at the window, then at the gloves,
> and then at her—and so on alternately.
>
> I found I lost considerably in every attack—she had a quick
> black eye, and shot through two such long and silken eye-lashes

with such penetration, that she looked into my very heart and reins—It may seem strange, but I could actually feel she did——It is no matter, said I, taking up a couple of the pairs next me, and putting them into my pocket.

I was sensible the beautiful *grisette* had not asked a single *livre* above the price—I wished she had asked a *livre* more, and was puzzling my brains how to bring the matter about— Do you think, my dear Sir, said she, mistaking my embarrassment, that I could ask a *sou* too much of a stranger—and of a stranger whose politeness, more than his want of gloves, has done me the honor to lay himself at my mercy?—*M'en croyez capable?*—Faith! not I, said I; and if you were, you are welcome. (pp. 102-103)

Yorick still is unable to practice the lesson of benevolence he learned at Calais. From the time he took leave of the Monk, all his expectations of courtesy, generosity, and fellow-feeling have been frustrated by his own egoistic lusts or his moral short-sightedness.

Yorick's experience at the Opéra Comique, when he goes there after leaving the glove shop, offers every opportunity to correct his errors; but Yorick is yet inadequate to the accomplishment. "There was nobody in the box I was let into but a kindly old French officer," and since Yorick has a predilection for old soldiers, he seats himself next the man. This old gentleman at once closes his book and removes his spectacles, an action which Yorlick "translates" to mean a welcome to one who is obviously a stranger and alone. Yorick in turn makes the old gentleman a bow—which means, he is "sensible of his attention, and returned him a thousand thanks for it." The exchange seems to be a simple case of unalloyed kindness, but Yorick's self-concern asserts itself immediately. He can only think of his own delicate abilities to "translate"—to render "the several turns of looks and limbs, with all their inflections and delineations, into plain words" (p. 105).[9] Furthermore, his illustration of the point is hardly in accord with the morality of the situation. He tells how he had translated the looks and manners of the Marquisina (*sic*) de F*** into an invitation to come home with her, adding "that the connection which arose out of the translation, gave me more

[9]Compare Sermon XLIII: "Nature has assigned a different look, tone of voice, and gesture, peculiar to every passion and affectation we are subject to; and, therefore, to argue against this strict correspondence which is held between our souls and bodies,—is disputing against the frame and mechanism of human nature" (Vol. II, pp. 344-345).

pleasure than any one I had the honor to make in Italy." The old man's kindness has only led Yorick to congratulate himself upon an illicit conquest.[10]

The two men then notice a dwarf in the *parterre* whose view of the stage is cut off by a giant German who will not move, and when asked only insults the little man. "An injury sharpened by an insult, be it to who it will, makes every man of sentiment a party; I could have leaped out of the box to have redressed it." The old officer is more suave; he beckons to a sentinel, who quickly forces the German to change places with the dwarf. Yorick is joyful at the outcome; yet it only leads to a tiff with the old gentleman: "And yet you would not permit this, said the old officer, in England.—In England, dear Sir, said I, *we sit all at our ease*" (pp. 112-113).

But national pride is not deep in this generous man, and when Yorick is scandalized by "an illiberal sarcasm at the church" offered by the entire audience, he is able to explain with frankness. An *abbé* has made the mistake of sitting down behind a couple of *grisettes*;

[10]I am taking liberties with the narrative point of view in my interpretation of the story of the Marquisina de F***, as well as with the story of Madame de Rambouliet which follows. I treat both tales as evidence that Yorick cannot react in an admirable way to the kindness and wisdom of the officer. It is only by a loose construction, however, that I can speak of them as parts of a chain of thoughts in Yorick's mind while at the Opéra. By a stricter construction, it is only as the narrator speaking from a later point in time that Yorick can bring in these stories, because at the time he goes to the Opéra and sits with the officer, he has not made the acquaintance of either lady. If the *Journey* is a confessional, one ought to distinguish between the "protagonist-Yorick," who makes many errors, and the older, wiser "narrator-Yorick," who looks back upon his former self, cognizant of his mistakes. However, such a narrator may retain some of the faults he recognizes in his earlier self. Consequently, to illustrate a point about how he once acted, he may say, "I am such and such a sort of person." In my interpretation, the "narrator-Yorick" speaks in this manner when he tells these stories. He means to indicate the *type* of reaction he had to the officer's remarks—a reaction which blocked his appreciation of the man. But the "narrator-Yorick" shows, in the book as a whole, a wisdom and balance much advanced over his state at the time of the actual journey; that he admires the old officer is patent in his narrative. His telling of stories out of keeping with the situation and pointing in a direction quite away from the morality of the officer implies, therefore, a fault in Yorick at the time of the actual meeting. See the interesting analysis of Tristram's four "selves," their relation to Sterne's concept of time and to the digressions, in Charles Parish's article, "The Nature of Mr. Tristram's Shandy, Author," *Boston University Studies in English*, V (1961), 74-90.

voices throughout the hall cry, "*Haussez les mains, Monsieur l'Abbé.*"
Yorick is shocked: "Good God! said I, turning pale with astonishment
—is it possible, that a people so smit with sentiment should at the
same time be so unclean, and so unlike themselves—*Quelle gros-
sièreté!*" (p. 114). The old officer then makes a comment of such
excellent good sense one would think it just the wisdom for which
a moral investigator might be searching:

> Every nation . . . have their refinements and *grossièretés*, in which
> they take the lead, and lose it of one another by turns. . . .
> *Le* POUR, *et le* CONTRE *se trouvent en chaque nation*; there is a
> balance, said he, of good and bad everywhere; and nothing but
> the knowing it is so can emancipate one half of the world from
> the prepossessions which it holds against the other—that the
> advantage of travel, as it regarded the *sçavoir vivre*, was by seeing
> a great deal both of men and manners; it taught us mutual
> toleration; and mutual toleration, concluded he, making me a
> bow, taught us mutual love. (p. 115)

Yorick's reaction is telling. The speech makes such good sense that
he first thinks he "loved the man." On second thought, however, he
decides, no, it is his own way of thinking—just better expressed. It
is ridiculous, of course, for Yorick to appropriate this wisdom to
himself when he has just revealed his prejudice that the French are
"smit with sentiment"; he is not able to understand how they can
be "so unlike themselves." But having distracted his attention away
from the officer's point to himself, he digresses upon a contingency
and thereby further flatters his own ego: he concentrates upon the
idea that in time we get used to foreign customs which at first seem
gross, illustrating the thought with the most delicate scatological tale
in English fiction:

> Madame de Rambouliet, after an acquaintance of about six
> weeks with her, had done me the honor to take me in her coach
> about two leagues out of town—Of all women, Madame de
> Rambouliet is the most correct; and I never wish to see one of
> more virtues and purity of heart—In our return back, Madame
> de Rambouliet desired me to pull the cord—I asked her if she
> wanted anything—*Rien que pisser*, said Madame de Ram-
> bouliet—
> Grieve not, gentle traveler, to let Madame de Rambouliet
> p—ss on—And, ye fair mystic nymphs! go each one *pluck your*

rose, and scatter them in your path—for Madame de Rambouliet did no more—I handed Madame de Rambouliet out of the coach; and had I been the priest of the chaste Castalia, I could not have served at her fountain with a more respectful decorum.   (pp. 116-117)

As a moral investigator, a searcher after benevolence, Yorick is still a failure at the close of the first volume.

Sterne's method of humor in this part of the *Journey* does not differ radically from that of *Tristram Shandy*. The key to personality in the longer novel had been the obsession—Walter's devotion to a hypothesis, Uncle Toby's miniature fortifications. The ruling passion of each brother sets his mind on one track, and all experience is made to serve that train of thought. They tend to discover confirmations of their pet notions everywhere, distorting reality by imparting to it a subjective, hobby-horsical vision of order. In the *Sentimental Journey*, Yorick too suffers from a monomania—he tends to see benevolence in every act, including the amoral and immoral; or he distorts true goodness, such as that of the old officer, allowing his mind to wander from the point and failing to understand. Benevolence is Yorick's hobby-horse.

The blindness of Yorick is not to be confused with the sensibility of his author. Critically considered by itself alone, the *Sentimental Journey* is far more than a mere exudation of sentimental emotions. And historically regarded, Laurence Sterne had a coolness toward French manners and a loyalty to English customs not at all suggestive of Yorick's predisposition. It may well be that Sterne first departed for France with many prepossessions in favor of French urbanity, but six months after his arrival, he was writing, "The humor is over for France, and Frenchmen" (*Letters*, p. 181). A few weeks later he wrote again, "the groundwork of my *ennui* is more to the eternal platitude of the French characters—little variety, no originality in it at all—than to any other cause—for they are very civil—but civility itself, in that uniform, wearies and bothers one to death" (*Letters*, p. 186). After a two-year stay, he was thoroughly sick of the place. "I am preparing, my dear Mrs. F., to leave France," he wrote on February 1, 1764, "for I am heartily tired of it—That insipidity there is in French characters has disgusted your friend Yorick" (*Letters*, p. 209). And the *London Chronicle* for April 16-18, 1765 (p. 373), reported the following "pleasant anecdote" about Sterne in Paris: "A French gentleman asked him, if he had found in

France no original characters that he could make use of in his history? *No,* replied he, *The French resemble old pieces of coin, whose impression is worn out by rubbing."* [11]

Still, along with an understandable yearning to be home and a loyalty to his own people, Sterne had a level-headed tolerance of foreign customs which he was to project into the character of the old officer at the Opéra Comique. Using a phrase he later put into the mouth of the officer, he wrote from Montpellier during the winter of 1763-1764, "I'm more than half tired of France, as fine a country as it is—but there is the *Pour* and the *Contre* for every place, all which being balanced, I think old England preferable to any kingdom in the world" (*Letters,* p. 201).

In fact, Sterne the historic man had a bit of Smelfungus in himself. He sent to his daughter, Lydia, a comment about the insincerity of French manners quite parallel to Smollett's remark in the *Travels* that the French, for all their suavity "are the least capable of feeling for the distresses of their fellow creatures." In the fall of 1767, when Sterne was completing the *Journey* and looking forward with mixed feelings to the return of Lydia and her mother, he wrote the daughter, "I will show you more real *politesses* than any you have met with in France, as mine will come warm from the heart" (*Letters,* p. 391).[12]

[11]Sterne used the image twice in the *Sentimental Journey* to give distant hints at his displeasure with the French character. In the glove shop he hints, thus, at the insensibility of the *grisette*: she is one of those French shopkeepers' wives who, "by a continual higgling with customers . . . like so many rough pebbles shook long together in a bag, by amicable collisions . . . have worn down their asperities and sharp angles, and not only become round and smooth, but will receive, some of them, a polish like a brilliant" (p. 99). In a later scene with the Comte de Bissy, Yorick uses the inverse image to describe the English, who "like ancient medals, kept more apart, and passing but few people's hands, preserve the first sharpness which the fine hand of nature has given them." Yorick at this point has actually laid some worn coins on the table before the Count, but at the moment we expect him to draw the comparison of the old coins to the French people, he suppresses the image: "But the French . . . are a loyal, a gallant, a generous, an ingenious, and good-tempered people as is under heaven—if they have a fault—they are too serious" (pp. 165-166).

[12]Sterne hated the thought that his daughter might become a French coquette: "I hope you have not forgot my last request," he wrote Lydia, "to make no friendships with the French women—not that I think ill of them all, but sometimes women of the best principles are the most *in-*

His worries were justified, for his wife's continental affectations, when she got home, so sickened Sterne that he could hardly finish the book. To a friend he wrote on December 3,

> In three weeks I shall kiss your hand—and sooner, if I can finish my Sentimental Journey.—The deuce take all sentiments! I wish there was not one in the world!—My wife is come to pay me a sentimental visit as far as from Avignon—and the *politesses* arising from such a proof of her urbanity, has robbed me of a month's writing, or I had been in town now.—I am going to lie-in; being at Christmas at my full reckoning—and unless what I shall bring forth is not [*sic*] *pressed* to death by these devils of printers, I shall have the honor of presenting to you a *couple of as clean brats* as ever chaste brain conceived—they are frolicsome too, *mais cela n'empêche pas*—. (*Letters*, p. 405)

It seems obvious Sterne had a clear notion what he would do with the *Sentimental Journey*. Smollett had given the impression of a traveler with a jaundiced eye who saw every act as meanness or greed. Sterne would create a character with rose-colored glasses who would find love and sympathy at every hand because he was determined to find them. Sterne's "frolicsome, clean brats" would not give the lie direct to Smollett. Sterne was more subtle than that; and besides he had a certain sympathy for the opinions of his old enemy.[13] He would set Yorick at an opposite extreme from Smelfungus but make him, in his own way, equally injudicious. Eventually, however, he would allow Yorick to learn a modicum of discrimination. Although he never in his journey discovers the whole of morality, Yorick does become aware of the distinction between *politesse* and *politesse de coeur*: in the second volume, he says to the comte de Bissy,

> A polished nation . . . makes everyone its debtor; and besides, urbanity itself, like the fair sex, has so many charms, it goes against the heart to say it can do ill; and yet . . . should it ever be the case of the English, in the progress of their refinements, to

---

sinuating—nay I am so jealous of you that I should be miserable were I to see you had the least grain and coquetry in your composition" (*Letters*, p. 212). See also *Letters*, p. 258, for another comment about French women.

   [13]Smollett's *Critical Review* had become increasingly critical of the various installments of *Tristram Shandy* and had strongly abused Sterne for publishing his sermons under the name "Mr. Yorick." See *Tristram Shandy*, pp. 161-162.

arrive at the same polish which distinguishes the French, if we did not lose the *politesse de coeur*, which inclines men more to humane actions, than courteous ones, we should at least lose that distinct variety and originality of character, which distinguishes them, not only from each other, but from all the world besides. (p. 165)

The lesson has cost Yorick some embarrassing disappointments, but at least he knows that urbanity can "do ill" and is not to be confused with "humane actions."

The chief difficulty of Yorick's moral experiment lies, not with the French people, who have their *pour* as well as their *contre*, but with Yorick himself. Sterne early drops such a hint in the preface, which he has Yorick write sitting in symbolic isolation in a one-man carriage called a *désobligeant*. Yorick there speculates upon how, not only ignorance of language and custom will stand in the way of the sentimental traveler, but his own enthusiasm as well. He illustrates the point with a playful paraphrase of *Genesis* 9:20-24, the story of Noah's drunkenness in his vineyard. Yorick's version concerns that Dutchman who first transplanted Burgundian grapes to the Cape of Good Hope. This man, Yorick writes, faced a special danger in his experiment quite aside from the exigencies of chance—the danger of himself. "By an intemperate confidence in the fortitude of his head, and the depth of his discretion, *Mynheer* might possibly overset both in his new vineyard; and by discovering his nakedness, become a laughing-stock to his people" (pp. 16-17). So with Yorick—by an intemperate confidence in a harvest of lovely sentiments, he gets drunk on imaginary moral goodness and becomes a laughing-stock.

Chapter II

BLIND PSYCHIC FORCES

According to Elizabeth Carter, Sterne's notion of benevolence was no more than a "substitute for virtue" which tended to "confound all differences of right and wrong." Thus Mrs. Carter, who refused herself to read the *Sentimental Journey*, reported what she had heard about it to Elizabeth Vesey. "Merely to be struck by a sudden impulse of compassion at the view of an object of distress," she concluded, "is no more benevolence than it is a fit of the gout." [1] Although they did not much appreciate Sterne's humor, the Bluestocking ladies did grasp the central dilemma of Sterne's book. They were right that Yorick's impulses of pity and sympathy toward particular objects did not measure up to the noble visions of benevolence then popular—such as Hutcheson's "calm, universal benevolence." Yorick is laughable just because he is confused upon this point.

Although he is a clergyman, Yorick has no adequate notion of true moral virtue. In fact, he is positively mistaken. He thinks that by finding benevolent affections in their most simple form he will find moral virtue. In Vol. II he states his purpose to the Comte de Bissy when he replies to a jesting question about his interest in French women:

> But I could wish, continued I, to spy the *nakedness* of their hearts, and through the different disguises of customs, climates, and religion, find out what is good in them to fashion my own by—and therefore am I come.
>
> . . . I conceive every fair being as a temple, and would rather enter in, and see the original drawings and loose sketches hung up in it, than the Transfiguration of Raphael itself.
>
> The thirst of this, continued I, as impatient as that which inflames the breast of the connoisseur, has led me from my own home into France—and from France will lead me through Italy

[1] *A Series of Letters between Mrs. Elizabeth Carter and Miss Catherine Talbot . . .*, ed. Montagu Pennington (London, 1809), Vol. III, 335.

—'tis a quiet journey of the heart in pursuit of NATURE, and those affections which rise out of her, which make us love each other—and the world, better than we do.   (pp. 155-156)

Notice Yorick's series of equivalents: he seeks the heart, the natural and lovely heart, which amounts to Nature, the source of affections of love. Yorick is looking for the natural affections he had called benevolence in the sermons. Yet he thinks they will provide an adequate model by which to fashion his own heart. He implies, thus, that the kindly affections constitute, if not the whole of virtue, at least an efficient cause of virtue. And in this implication Yorick departs from the sermons of his author, Laurence Sterne.

Yorick is confused. Mrs. Carter and her friends were confused. But I doubt that Sterne was. Moralists of Sterne's time had come to recognize that limited and particular impulses, no matter how amiable, fall short of true virtue. I believe Sterne was having fun with this doctrine, so common to the ethical writing of his time.

The notion of natural benevolence, as the studies of Ronald Crane and Rae Blanchard have shown, was widespread and popular during the late seventeenth and early eighteenth centuries. Many moralists, especially those liberal Anglican divines called "Latitudinarians," rebelled against the old Stoic doctrine that the reason should completely subdue the passion. They defended human affection and lauded man's native compassion and generosity. These clergymen remained rationalists, however, holding to their belief that reason must keep the control over passion, allowing the morally beneficial affection room, but curtailing the harmful. Up to Sterne's time a great many clergymen continued to think in this way.

However, the attacks upon their position by Francis Hutcheson and David Hume appear to have forced the more thoughtful rationalists into a careful explanation of the relationship between passion and reason. These two "sentimental" moralists had worked out an ethic in which reason was subordinate to affection.[2] As a result, the rationalists became cautious in their praise of benevolence. Bishop Butler, who won the respect of succeeding ages by his clear proof that man indeed has instinctive benevolence, also insisted that "benevolence, and the want of it, singly considered, are in no sort the whole

[2]Hutcheson, *Inquiry into the Original of our Ideas of Beauty and Virtue . . .*, 1725; and *Essay on the Nature and Conduct of the Passions and Affections. With Illustrations on the Moral Sense*, 1728. Hume, *Treatise of Human Nature*, 1739-40; and *Enquiry Concerning the Principles of Morals*, 1751.

of virtue and vice." [3] The implication in Butler's argument is well put by his nineteenth-century follower, James Martineau: "A Force, simply as such, is no moral object at all. Nor does it make the least difference in this respect that it is put *inside* an organism to work from the centre, instead of *outside*. ... The dynamics of living beings are as foreign to ethics as the gravitation of the stars." [4] However, the attitude and the image had both been expressed in the eighteenth century. In 1740 George Turnbull had argued that "the benevolent principle in our nature" cannot be the essence of virtue because it is only another force like "attractions in the material system." [5]

Rational moralists did not deny the existence of this benevolent force; they simply insisted it was not a moral entity. John Balguy, in his criticism of Hutcheson, wrote, "That the Author of Nature has planted in our minds benevolent affections towards others, cannot be denied without contradicting experience, and falsifying our own impressions." But such emotions are "in a moral sense, worthless. If it be said that instincts do not *force* the mind, but only *incline* it; I answer, that as much room as they leave for the use of liberty and the exercise of reason, so much room they leave for virtue." [6]

Whether or not Sterne was familiar with the authors here cited, we cannot know. Nevertheless, the moralists point to a central element of his comedy: benevolent affections, which have the superficial appearance of morality actualized, turn out to be no more than mechanical forces. The sermons appear to confirm this interpretation. "Tenderness and disinterested compassion," Sterne writes in Sermon VII are a "bias" of nature which shows most clearly in children, who

[3] "Dissertation II." appended to *Analogy of Religion*, in *Works*, ed. W. E. Gladstone (Oxford: Clarendon, 1896), Vol. I, 407. *Cf.* Sermon XII, Vol. II, 209 ff.

[4] *Types of Ethical Theory* (Oxford: Clarendon, 1891), Vol. II, 33.

[5] *Principles of Moral Philosophy* ... (London, 1740), p. 190.

[6] *The Foundation of Moral Goodness*, 1728, in *A Collection of Tracts, Moral and Theological* (London, 1734), pp. 45, 58. See also William Adams, *The Nature and Obligation of Virtue* (London, 1754), p. 10: "As God has implanted many passions and good affections in the mind to excite us to duty, whatever good we do from these principles, and not from reason, so much is lost of the merit and virtue of the action." Again in Richard Price, *A Review of the Principal Questions in Morals*, 1757, ed. recently by D. Daiches Raphael (Oxford: Clarendon, 1948), p. 191: "But *instinctive benevolence* is no principle of virtue, nor are any actions flowing merely from it virtuous. As far as this influences, so far something else than reason and goodness influences, and so much I think is to be subtracted from the moral worth of any action or character."

have "come out of the hands of God" with their propensities untrammeled (Vol. I, p. 117). Such an original impulse does appear to be automatic: there is "something in our nature which engages us to take part in every accident to which man is subject . . . so that without any observable act of the will, we suffer with the unfortunate" (Vol. I, pp. 38-39). If Elizabeth Carter had in mind scenes such as Yorick's relieving the beggars at Calais, she is right that the pity and sympathy are more like "a fit of the gout" than like Christian charity.[7]

But some of Sterne's comedy goes beyond merely presenting a mechanical benevolence. If it is really no more than an instinct, benevolence surely can become pernicious under some circumstances. That was an argument made by a little-known writer, John Taylor, ten years before the appearance of the *Sentimental Journey*: (1) "We are all conscious, that benevolence, sympathy, or social affections are instincts implanted in our nature." (2) But "*Instinct* is the mechanism of an animal, which hath the same effect upon its motions, as weights and springs upon the motions of a machine, moving, impelling, exciting or determining the animal involuntarily, or without thought and reflection." Consequently, (3) "benevolence may act in vicious as well as virtuous characters, when weakened and overpowered, or misled by opinion or imagination; and therefore is so far from constituting actions morally good, that it may be the ground of actions morally evil." [8]

To transcend the natural or conditioned admiration for benevolent conduct, to see the possibility that in some circumstances sympathy, kindness, generosity can become "the ground of actions morally evil," required an admirable devotion to logic on the part of John Taylor, albeit he won no lasting place in the history of philosophy. Sterne, in all probability, arrived at his own view empirically, rather than logically. Nevertheless, his novels reflect the growing eighteenth-century awareness that time-honored doctrines and trite responses do not necessarily reveal the moral truth. The paradox Laurence Sterne

[7]My point has been anticipated by Alan McKillop in *Early Masters of English Fiction* (Lawrence: University of Kansas Press, 1956), p. 216: "Extreme sentiment has this in common with the humors, that it may be taken as a mechanical force getting out of control, and so has its ridiculous side. Sterne realizes this principle, and uses it throughout his work for comic effect. . . ."

[8]*An Examination of the Scheme of Morality, Advanced by Dr. Hutcheson* (London, 1759), pp. 20-21, 34.

made central to his sentimental comedy amounts to the argument predicted by John Taylor—benevolence can be vicious.

This paradox is apparent in Yorick's flirtation with the charming Fleming, Madame de L***, in the Calais scenes. His first meeting with her comes about accidentally when he is dickering for a coach. Yorick, scolding himself for the greed he senses while driving a bargain, turns suddenly, muttering, "base, ungentle passion! thy hand is against every man, and every man's hand against thee." He almost collides with the lady as he turns. If every man's hand is against greed, not every woman's; for when Yorick offers the lady his, she accepts. Monsieur Dessein, the innkeeper, discovering at this moment that he has the wrong key to the *remise*, disappears, leaving the hand-holding strangers comically facing the locked door.

Here Yorick interrupts the narrative to explain the moral import of his experience: "But what were the temptations (as I write not to apologize for the weaknesses of my heart in this tour—but to give an account of them)—shall be described with the same simplicity, with which I felt them" (p. 25). The subsequent chapter called "The Remise Door" has been frequently misunderstood by critics who lose sight of the fact that it is an account of Yorick's brush with sin. "Such," he specifies at its conclusion, "were my temptations" (p. 28).

Yorick's temptations amount to two ill-founded rationalizations (to use modern jargon) by which he can hide from himself the sexual impulse behind his attentions to this handsome woman: he convinces himself (1) that she is of a "high order" of beings worthy of his sympathy, and (2) that she suffers from some untold misfortune. The impression of her high quality, he tells us, had first occurred when he had caught an earlier glimpse of her talking with the Monk about, Yorick had supposed, his rudeness to that man. "Something jarred upon it within me—I wished him at his convent. When the heart flies out before the understanding, it saves the judgment a world of pains—I was certain she was a better order of beings" (p. 26).[9] The impression of the lady's quality returns while he is standing with her: "a guarded frankness with which she gave me her hand, showed, I

[9]Ernest A. Baker, in *The History of the English Novel*, Vol. IV (London: H. F. and G. Witherby, 1930), 260, cites the line, "When the heart flies out before the understanding, it saves the judgment a world of pains," as evidence that Sterne "inculcates obedience to the feelings alone." In the particular instance, certainly, Yorick's heart rules his head. But Yorick is confessing the events which led to a temptation. The heart's rule of the head is Yorick's human weakness, not Sterne's philosophy of life.

thought, her good education and her good sense." Yet Yorick has made this judgment without once seeing her face. What need? That "seduced and seducing slut," Fancy, has provided all Yorick wants. Consequently, when he does look at her face, he discovers that which will justify his attentions—her distress: "I fancied it wore the characters of a widowed look, and in that state of its declension, which had passed the two first paroxysms of sorrow, and was quietly beginning to reconcile itself to its loss" (pp. 27-28). These imagined premises, that the lady is of good breeding and in distress provide the mask for Yorick's animal desire. He calls them his "system":

> Having, on first sight of the lady, settled the affair in my fancy, "that she was of the better order of beings"—and then laid it down as a second axiom, as indisputable as the first, That she was a widow, and wore a character of distress—I went no further; I got ground enough for the situation which pleased me—and had she remained close beside my elbow till midnight, I should have held true to my system, and considered her only under that general idea.   (p. 39)

Eventually Yorick learns that his "system" is sound, for Madame de L*** is a person of quality distressed by widowhood. But Yorick is clear about the fact that he could not have been certain of these axioms at the time. He "went no further" than what "pleased" him. It is irrational "Fancy" which constructs an object suited to call forth the affection Yorick seeks.

Having established that much, Sterne can make the paradoxical point central to the comedy: "In a word," says Yorick, "I felt benevolence for her; and resolved some way or other to throw in my mite of courtesy—if not of service" (p. 28). Benevolence has become part of Yorick's temptation to the sin of carnality.[10]

Although Yorick need not blame his sexual desires, which in their mechanical nature are innocent, he is called upon to judge their tendency to lead him into an act prohibited by the moral law. He reveals such an awareness in his comment that there are "worthier occasions" than this flirtation (p. 30). He must, therefore, trick himself, he must allow the heart to fly before the understanding, the fancy before the fact. Thus the mechanical force of benevolence becomes, in this context, vicious in the sense that its misdirected energy impels Yorick in the direction of a sinful act.

[10]The pun on the word *service* recalls the "cock and bull story" with which Sterne ended *Tristram Shandy*.

We must not think, however, that Yorick's benevolence is feigned. Madame de L*** herself makes clear that he is genuinely concerned to help her: "A man, my good Sir, has seldom an offer of kindness to make to a woman, but she has a presentiment of it some moments before." Yorick, aware of her trust tries to be frank about the desires he vaguely senses: "Nature arms her with it [presentiment] . . . for immediate preservation." The lady, however, will not accept a suggestion that Yorick could have intended any mischief:

> But I think, said she, looking in my face, I had no evil to apprehend—and to deal frankly with you, had determined to accept it [Yorick's offer].—If I had—(she stopped a moment)—I believe your good will would have drawn a story from me, which would have made pity the only dangerous thing in the journey. (pp. 47-48)

Yorick's pity is real enough, but no more real than his lust.

It is possible that Sterne's paradox of benevolence becoming vicious when associated with sexual desire was suggested by the moral literature of his time. Of course, we cannot and need not be certain he had a particular "source." Curiously, however, the "sentimental" school of philosophers used an argument suggestive of Sterne's treatment of sex and sentiment in the *Journey*. These thinkers frequently argued for the existence of natural benevolence by showing its presence in situations where it was least expected. One such argument maintained that it could be found in all attachments between the sexes. In fact, the moralists thought that no attraction between men and women could be strong unless reinforced with feelings of good-will. Shaftesbury maintained that the power of beauty cannot sustain love without the aid of "tenderness and generosity of affection." Such is the case, he thought, even when the liaison is grossly immoral:

> The courtesans, and even the commonest of women, who live by prostitution, know very well how necessary it is that everyone whom they entertain with their beauty should believe there are satisfactions reciprocal, and that pleasures are no less given than received.[11]

Francis Hutcheson made a similar point. In illicit love,

> a mixture of the moral pleasures is what gives the alluring relish; 'tis some appearance of friendship, of love, of communicating

[11]*Characteristics of Men, Manners, Opinions, Times*, ed. John M. Robertson (London: Grant Richards, 1900), Vol. I, 310-311.

pleasure to others, which preserves the pleasures of the luxurious from being nauseous and insipid.

Beauty of person itself, thinks Hutcheson, is not determined by the physical, but by "some apprehended morality." Furthermore, he argues, if sensual pleasure were the chief motive to debauchery or false gallantry,

> the meanest prostitutes would please as much as any. But we know sufficiently, that men are fond of good-nature, faith, pleasantry of temper, wit, and many other moral qualities, even in a mistress. And this may furnish us with a reason for what appears pretty unaccountable, *viz.* that chastity itself has a powerful charm in the eyes of the dissolute, even when they are attempting to destroy it.[12]

Madame de L*** is hardly a mean woman, and Yorick is no gross sensualist. The point is that these two are attracted to each other illicitly as much out of feelings of good-will as out of sexual desire. "Love between the sexes," wrote David Hume, "begets a complacency and good-will very distinct from the gratification of an appetite." [13] But a lesser-known sentimental moralist, David Fordyce, provides a more detailed description of the sort of attraction Yorick has for Madame de L***:

> When our friendship terminates on any of the other sex, in whom beauty or agreeableness of person and external gracefulness of manners conspire to express and heighten the moral charm of a tender honest heart; and sweet, ingenious, modest temper, lighted up by good sense, it generally grows into a more soft and endearing attachment. ... it becomes the source of many amiable duties, of a communication of passions and interests, of the most refined decencies, and of a thousand nameless, deep-felt joys of reciprocal tenderness and love, flowing from every look, word, and action. Here friendship acts with double energy, and the natural conspires with the moral charm, to strengthen and secure the love of virtue.[14]

[12]*Inquiry into the Original of our Ideas of Beauty and Virtue* (London, 1738), pp. 250, 258.

[13]*Enquiry Concerning the Principles of Morals* in *Enquiries*, ed. L. A. Selby-Bigge (Oxford: Clarendon, 1902), p. 300.

[14]"Elements of Moral Philosophy," in *The Preceptor*, ed. Robert Dodsley (London, 1748), Vol. II, 319-320. Cf. *Tristram Shandy*, p. 49: "Surely, Madam, a friendship between the two sexes may subsist, and be

Even in the serious discussions of the moral philosophers, something is apt to strike us as comic in the idea of sexual passions working in cooperation with benevolence. We come close to smiling when we read Hutcheson's explanation that love makes us expect, "the greatest moral pleasures along with the sensible, and a thousand tender sentiments of humanity and generosity; and makes us impatient for a society which we imagine big with unspeakable pleasures." [15] Sterne alters the idea hardly at all, but draws out of it the implicit comedy. Yorick, looking forward to a sentimental assignation with Madame de L***, exclaims,

> With what a moral delight will it crown my journey, in sharing in the sickening incidents of a tale of misery told to me by such a sufferer? To see her weep! and though I cannot dry up the fountain of her tears, what an exquisite sensation is there still left, in wiping them away from off the cheeks of the first and fairest of women, as I'm sitting with my handkerchief in my hand in silence the whole night beside her. (pp. 78-79)

Yet Sterne goes to a further extreme even than this. If benevolence is so closely allied to sex, it is Yorick's duty to stay in love at all times:

> ... having been in love with one princess or other almost all my life, and I hope I shall go on so till I die, being firmly persuaded, that if ever I do a mean action, it must be in some interval betwixt one passion and another: whilst this interregnum lasts, I always perceive my heart locked up—I can scarce find in it, to give Misery a sixpence: and therefore I always get out of it as fast as I can, and the moment I am rekindled, I am all generosity and good will again; and would do anything in the world either for, or with anyone, if they will but satisfy me there is no sin in it. (p. 62)

Yet here too the moralists had set a precedent. Yorick's declaration,

---

supported without—Fy! Mr. Shandy:——Without anything, Madam, but that tender and delicious sentiment, which ever mixes in friendship, where there is a difference of sex. Let me intreat you to study the pure and sentimental parts of the best French romances;—it will really, Madam, astonish you to see with what a variety of chaste expression this delicious sentiment, which I have the honor to speak of, is dressed out."

[15] *Inquiry,* p. 257.

which strikes us as the ridiculous extremity of his laughable moral vision, had been approximated by David Hume:

> An affection betwixt the sexes is a passion evidently implanted in human nature; and this passion not only appears in its peculiar symptoms, but also in inflaming every other principle of affection, and raising a stronger love from beauty, wit, kindness, than what would otherwise flow from them.[16]

Sterne, the comic writer, brings to the idea no more than a slight confounding of means and ends by allowing Yorick's sexual love to serve as the means to benevolence—the law of chastity, of course, defining a line he must not overstep. In love, as anything else, Yorick rides his hobby.

But he is not to be taken as that more common literary figure— the hypocrite. If he distorts reality, it is not to take advantage of women, but to release feelings of love and pity. If we deny the reality of those impulses, as did Thackeray, Yorick will seem a lecherous priest; if we ignore the strength of his sexual drives, as did Walter Sichel, he will appear an enervated, sentimental "firefly." Both these views overlook the humor in the *Sentimental Journey*, and both deny its truth. But when we consider cooly, we must admit that pity and charity often keep company with desire. The philosophers had a convincing point, and Sterne wrote a convincing narrative.

The close association of benevolence with wantonness in the *Journey* implies, not that either is false, but that neither is moral. Sterne does not think any affection good or bad in itself alone. When he speaks, in the sermons, of good or vicious passions, he means only to indicate their general tendency toward virtuous or evil *acts*; but the moral worth of the act is determined by some standard outside the emotional constitution—by the law of God or the pronouncements of reason. We are here concerned with the problem of moral *character*, the disposition which leads a person to act in a moral way or to fail of such conduct. Judgments of moral character take account of the whole personality, not of individual instincts, which are always innocent just because they are mechanical. Self-love, for instance, Sterne says in Sermon XXXIV, is given for "preservation" and useful if controlled (Vol. II, p. 212). Covetousness he describes as leading to cruelty when unchecked, but "not naturally cruel in it-

---

[16]*A Treatise of Human Nature*, ed. L. A. Selby-Bigge (Oxford, 1896), p. 481 (III, ii, 1). *Cf. Tristram Shandy*, p. 578: "I call not love a misfortune, from a persuasion, that man's heart is ever the better for it."

self" (Vol. I, p. 306). Ambition, "though in general it was an irregular appetite, which in most cases, 'twas dangerous to gratify, yet in effect 'twas only so far criminal, as the power which it acquired was perverted to bad and vicious purposes" (Vol. I, p. 220). And when Sterne draws up a list of passions—pride, treachery, envy, hypocrisy, malice, cruelty, and self-love—he does not call them evil, but says that they are the "occasion" of evil (Vol. I, p. 183). It is Sterne's genius to see the comic possibilities in a common confusion between true moral worth and certain lovely, winning affections of benevolence, which are, nevertheless, amoral because they are mechanical.

On the other hand Sterne does make judgments about moral character. In doing so, however, he looks, not to individual instincts, but to the order and organization which the person has allowed to his impulses. All the instincts cry for satisfaction. Those which are indulged will grow strong and dominant in the personality; those which are denied will lose force and atrophy. Some passions are originally stronger than others and tend to "disorder" the personality or make it "irregular" (Vol. II, pp. 54, 127-128, 230). Order among the passions can be attained, however, and is a requisite to virtue—but not in itself a guarantee of virtue. This order we can best visualize as a pyramid, with one or a few emotions on top which dominate the others; in this particular, Sterne's position is about that of the old humor psychology. If the dominating appetite or impulse is one which Sterne thinks is apt to encourage evil, he usually calls it a "ruling passion." In Sermon IX, he argues that one cannot judge the character of Herod by simply balancing out his good and evil qualities like a bookkeeper. The important point to settle in judging Herod is the order of rule and subordination which permits "so many different attempts to gratify the same governing appetite," which is for Herod greed (Vol. I, p. 148).[17] In another sermon he makes, in passing, a general stricture of everyone who adopts as much morality and religion "as will least interfere with his principal and ruling passion" (Vol. I, p. 175).

A man of truly moral character, however, has an emotional make-up which tends toward virtuous actions. In describing such a personality, Sterne usually avoids the term *ruling passion*, using in its place the word *temper*. And in such descriptions he is apt to borrow

[17]In Sermon XIX Sterne says that in most instances greed is "subordinate and ministerial" to some other passion such as ambition—in which case it would not be a ruling passion (Vol. I, p. 308).

the rhetoric of the Latitudinarians in claiming a high degree of naturalness for the virtuous temper. One of the fullest expressions of his ideal is found in Sermon XLI, "Follow Peace."

> The great end and design of our holy religion, next to the main view of reconciling us to God, was to reconcile us to each other; —by teaching us to subdue all those unfriendly dispositions in our nature, which unfit us for happiness, and the social enjoyment of the many blessings which God has enabled us to partake of in this world, miserable as it is, in many respects.— Could Christianity persuade the professors of it into this temper, and engage us, as its doctrine requires, to go on and exalt our natures, and, after the subduction of the most unfriendly of our passions, to plant, in the room of them, all those (more natural to the soil) humane and benevolent inclinations, which, in imitation of the perfections of God, should dispose us to extend our love and goodness to our fellow-creatures, according to the extent of our abilities;—in like manner, as the goodness of God extends itself over all the works of the creation:—could this be accomplished,—the world would be worth living in. (Vol. II, pp. 313-314)[18]

In Sermon III Sterne takes his ideal a step further. The man so conditioned that the benevolent affections dominate all appetites and instincts will be inclined, not only to keep the command of charity, but to practice all duties:

> 'Tis observable in many places of Scripture, that our blessed Saviour, in describing the day of judgment, does it in such a manner, as if the great inquiry then, was to relate principally to this one virtue of compassion—and as if our final sentence at that solemnity was to be pronounced exactly according to the degree of it. . . . Not that we are to imagine from thence, as if any other good or evil action should then be over-looked by the eye of the All-seeing Judge, but barely to intimate to us, that a charitable and benevolent disposition is so principal and ruling a part of a man's character, as to be a considerable test by itself of the whole frame and temper of his mind, with which all other

[18]Hammond, p. 114, cites Clarke as the source of this statement; but the words are not at all close to Clarke's. On p. 155, Hammond attributes the passage to Tillotson; there is some suggestion of Tillotson's wording in Sterne's statement, but I doubt that it is a direct plagiarism.

virtues and vices respectively rise and fall, and will almost necessarily be connected. (Vol. I, pp. 50-51)[19]

The developing of such a benevolent temper seems to be a hit-or-
miss affair.[20] Pushed this way and that by the passions, each person
must help himself as he can. Habit, however, is the cementing agent:
"our passions are apt to grow upon us by indulgence, and become
exorbitant" (Vol. II, p. 259).[21] If we do not take care the seeds of
vice with which we are born "insensibly grow up with us from our
childhood" (Vol. I, p. 66). If man's vicious inclinations are "strong
by nature," they are made "more so by uncontrolled custom" (Vol.
II, p. 318). On the other hand, people really accomplished in virtue
have "a settled principle of humanity and goodness," that is, benevolence has become habitual in them (Vol. I, p. 45). Every man must
work out his own economics of the passions. Through experience he
discovers and learns to avoid inclinations which have a "natural
connection" to others of an "unsocial aspect" (Vol. II, p. 51). Goodness can be attained, but only through rigorous self-discipline; it
comes to those "who sacrifice their appetites and passions from a
consciousness of their duty to God" (Vol. I, pp. 124-125). "The great
business of man," writes Sterne, "is the regulation of his spirit; the
possession of such a frame and temper of mind, as will lead us [*sic*]
peaceably through this world" (Vol. II, p. 59; also Vol. I, pp. 252-
253).[22]

[19]There can be little doubt that Sterne took the principal parts of this
statement from Clarke, as Hammond, p. 114, points out. But Hammond
also attributes it to Tillotson on p. 172.

[20]Ultimately, however, reason can initiate any change in the personality.
See below, Chapter V.

[21]Sterne's sentence is a "crib" from Wollaston's *Religion of Nature
Delineated*; see Hammond, p. 181.

[22]Sterne's psychology is suggestive of Robert Burton's *Anatomy of
Melancholy*, from which he borrowed so many passages of *Tristram
Shandy*. See for example the edition by Floyd Dell and Paul Jorden-
Smith (New York: Tudor, 1948), pp. 146-147: "... in voluntary things
we are averse from God and goodness, bad by nature, by ignorance
worse, by art, discipline, custom, we get many bad habits: suffering them
to domineer and tyrannize over us; and the devil is still ready at hand
with his evil suggestions ... except our *will* be swayed and counterpoised
again with some divine precepts, and good motions of the spirit, which
many times restrain, hinder, and check us, when we are in the full career
of our dissolute courses. So David corrected himself, when he had Saul
at a vantage. Revenge and malice were as two violent oppugners on the
one side; but honesty, religion, fear of God, withheld him on the other."

Sterne would have agreed with John Balguy that an instinct of pity or charity is "in a moral sense, worthless." That amiable tendency in man is so natural that even the most vile of men have some of it: the tyrant, Alexander of Pherae, wept at a tragedy because, Sterne says, when "all his vices were laid asleep;—then Nature awoke in triumph, and showed how deeply she had sown the seeds of compassion in every man's breast; when tyrants, with vices the most at enmity with it, were not able entirely to root it out" (Vol. I, p, 86).[23]

Yorick, who has his little egoistic impulses, is not obviously a bad man. But the fact that he also has benevolent "powers of nature, stirring within" (p. 68) does not make him obviously a good man. Taken as a whole, he falls short of Sterne's own ideal of the temper of goodness, a comic figure victimized by the conflicting "impulses which generally do determine me" (p. 59).

So far as I have been able to discover, Sterne's major departure from the ancient humor psychology represented by Burton is that he did not link personality types to the four bodily humors.

[23]The example is plagiarized from Wollaston—Hammond, p. 180.

Chapter III

THE MORAL FAILURE

The instinct psychology which Sterne visualized implies that the worth of a person's moral character depends, not on the mechanical impulses, but on the secondary motives with which he disciplines his passions. Beyond the original instinct or "movement," there are two general motive forces controllable at will. (1) The agent can act from a desire for pleasure. (2) Or he can permit an intellectual control arising from his looking to the consequences of his action upon the society or cosmos. Because these considerations involve a choice and are not merely mechanical, they must be scrutinized carefully in any judgment of moral character.[1]

All readers of the *Sentimental Journey* recognize that Yorick is engrossed in the pleasures of moral adventures and discoveries:

> —What a large volume of adventures may be grasped within this little span of life by him who interests his heart in everything, and who, having eyes to see, what time and chance are perpetually holding out to him as he journeyeth on his way, misses nothing he can *fairly* lay his hands on.—
> —If this won't turn out something—another will—no matter—'tis an essay upon human nature—I get my labor for my pains—'tis enough—the pleasure of the experiment has kept my senses, and the best part of my blood awake, and laid the gross to sleep. (pp. 49-50)

Such an attitude demands interpretation if we are to understand the moral implications of the novel.

[1]The rudiments of the following analysis were suggested by C. D. Broad's discussion of Bishop Joseph Butler in *Five Types of Ethical Theory* (London: Routledge and Kegan Paul, 1930), pp. 53-83. Sterne's ethic being less detailed and systematic than Butler's, I have occasion to use only a few simple concepts explained by Professor Broad. Sterne's ethic does not "closely" resemble that of Butler, but suggests it in broad outline.

69

The first distinction needed here is that between pleasure and happiness. Sterne's major comment on the matter is in the first sermon, "Inquiry after Happiness." He regards happiness as the "first and strongest" desire of man's nature. It is "only to be found in religion—in the consciousness of virtue—and the sure and certain hopes of a better life, which brightens all our prospects, and leaves no room to dread disappointments—because the expectation of it is built upon a rock whose foundations are as deep as those of heaven and hell" (Vol. I, p. 16). Happiness, it would seem, is a broad word applicable to the whole personality of a moral man. On the other hand, pleasure is particular and arises from the satisfaction of an instinct or desire. Although we seek pleasure, it puzzles us by the "insufficiency of the enjoyments." Sterne describes in detail the typical quests after pleasure in the forms of power, wealth, pomp, sensual delights, and (notably) scholarly study—all of which arise initially "from the common gratifications of our appetites, and the impressions of a thousand objects" (Vol. I, p. 16)—and all of which are vain.

One might, with some hesitation, call Sterne a eudaemonist, but never a hedonist. Sermons I, XXIII, and XXIX make the distinction between pleasure and happiness a major theme, and many others mention it. Again and again Sterne urges his parishioners "to provide for our true interest,—and do ourselves the most effectual service— by devoting ourselves to Him,—and always thinking of Him,—as He is the true and final happiness" (Vol. II, p. 294). In incidental passages too numerous to document, Sterne urges Christians to employ their thoughts on the next world with its promise of happiness (*e.g.*, Vol. I, pp. 124-125; Vol. II, pp. 138, 146, 158, 208). Significantly, he does not conclude his argument for the naturalness of benevolence, the "Vindication of Human Nature," with the advice that we should all relax and be natural. Instead Sterne emphasizes man's relation to God, begging his listeners to think upon the "just God overlooking, and the terror of an after-reckoning" which should lead to the sacrifice of many appetites and passions. True happiness depends upon God's justice, but the awareness of justice begets peace and contentment in a virtuous mind. This very orthodox doctrine is apparent upon almost every page of Sterne's sermons.

A question naturally arises at this point: what must one do to attain such happiness? The answer is equally orthodox—"Fear God and keep his commandments." This text for Sermon XXXIX is a frequent imperative in the homilies. It would be too simple to say that for Sterne virtue is virtue simply because God commands it; his rationalism precludes such a notion.[2] Nevertheless, the commands of God are positive and unerring measures of duty. Sterne is no theologian, and he raises no problems about the revelation of those commands. If he disputed the question of miracles with David Hume over the Ambassador's table, nothing on the question worthy of that philosopher's opposition ever found a way into the published sermons.[3] In the complacent way of so many clergy, he merely assumes that if one has his Bible at hand, he can learn what is rewardable in Heaven, what damnable in Hell. His interest is less in determining the content of the law of God than in disciplining ourselves to keep it.

Pleasure, as distinct from happiness, arises from the satisfaction of an instinct or appetite; the frustration of these impulses results in pain. This is so whether the instinct be one which leads to obedience of God or not. Thus goodness, which involves the checking of many natural instincts, can only be "got and maintained by a painful conflict and perpetual war against the passions" (Vol. I, p. 107). Yet evil too demands frustrations, in this case of the benevolent instincts, causing "great violence" and "many a painful conflict" in the wicked (Vol. I, pp. 49, 85).

Yorick's search for the pleasures of sentimental commerce has a sound psychological theory behind it. Yet one cannot argue that his desire for pleasure indicates that the benevolence he seeks and finds is a sham. The original blind impulse to pity or to aid another is in-

[2]Below, Chapter V.

[3]It is regrettable that we know so little about the friendship between the greatest sentimentalist of belles-lettres and the greatest philosopher of moral sentiments. Sterne included in the *Journey* an anecdote about Hume at a dinner in the English embassy in Paris (p. 54), probably the evening of their first meeting. The dispute over miracles probably took place at that time. Sterne described the disagreement in a letter, adding, "did I never meet with a being of a more placid and gentle nature; and it is this amiable turn of his character, that has given more consequence and force to his scepticism, than all the arguments of his sophistry" (*Letters*, p. 218). Hume, for his part, had an amusingly qualified admiration of Sterne. In a letter of 1773, he commented, "The best book, that has been writ by any Englishman these thirty years (for Dr. Franklin is an American) is *Tristram Shandy*, bad as it is"—*Letters of David Hume*, ed. J. Y. T. Grieg (Oxford: Clarendon, 1932), Vol. II, p. 269. For a summary of the known facts about the friendship, see Grieg's study, *David Hume* (New York: Oxford University Press, 1931), pp. 302-304.

dependent of any desire for pleasure. Benevolent youth, Sterne explains in Sermon VII, acts only "as it feels itself prompted by the inward workings of benevolence—without view to itself, or previous calculation either of the loss or profit which may accrue" (Vol. I, pp. 117-118). The only *object* to this instinctive response is the person in need of aid or compassion; pleasure cannot be the object, because the youth responds only to the pitiful person and situation.[4] Sterne is quite clear that the satisfaction of a benevolent impulse does bring pleasure, but only because it is man's nature to feel pleasure upon satisfying any impulse at all. Initially man is prompted by instinct. Secondarily, *after* he discovers that every satisfied passion brings pleasure, he may, if he chooses, act upon a secondary and learned motive—the desire for pleasure.

Sterne as a clergyman found nothing wrong with pleasure as such. He thought a good man could lead a very pleasant life (Vol. II, p. 250), and he could not tolerate the ascetic denial of joy. The "prejudice" which has done Christianity the most "dishonor" is the belief that "Christians are bound to make the worst of it, and tread it barefoot upon thorns and briars" (Vol. II, p. 253). In his discussion of Job in Sermon X, Sterne is forced to concede that the only absolutely certain reward is heaven. But in Sermon XXVIII, "Temporal Advantages of Religion," he struggles to show how goodness is rewarded by material prosperity and joy in this life. Even from the pulpit he seems to cry, "*En attendant—Vive l'amour! et vive la bagatelle!*"

> Consider, I beseech you, what provision and accommodation the
> Author of our being has prepared for us, that we might not go

[4]Hume explains the concept in the *Enquiry Concerning the Principles of Morals*, in *Enquiries*, ed. L. A. Selby-Bigge (Oxford: Clarendon, 1902), pp. 303-304: "The social virtues of humanity and benevolence exert their influence immediately by a direct tendency or instinct, which chiefly keeps in view the simple object, moving the affections, and comprehends not any scheme or system, nor the consequences resulting from the concurrence, imitation, or example to others. A parent flies to the relief of his child. . . . A generous man cheerfully embraces an opportunity of serving his friend; because he then feels himself under the dominion of the beneficent affections, nor is he concerned whether any other person in the universe were ever before actuated by such noble motives, or will ever afterwards prove their influence. In all these cases the social passions have in view a single individual object, and pursue the safety or happiness alone of the person loved or esteemed. With this they are satisfied: in this they acquiesce."

on our way sorrowing—how many caravanserais of rest—what powers and faculties he has given us for taking it—what apt objects he has placed in our way to entertain us;—some of which he has made so fair, so exquisitely fitted for this end, that they have power over us for a time to charm away the sense of pain, to cheer up the dejected heart under poverty and sickness, and make it go and remember its miseries no more.

. . . we are travelers, and, in most affecting sense of that idea, that like travelers, though upon business of the last and nearest concern to us, we may surely be allowed to amuse ourselves with the natural or artificial beauties of the country we are passing through, without reproach of forgetting the main errand we are sent upon; and if we can so order it, as not to be led out of the way, by the variety of prospects, edifices, and ruins which solicit us, it would be a nonsensical piece of saint-errantry to shut our eyes.

But Sterne adds a serious warning:

. . . let us not lose sight of the argument in pursuit of the simile.

Let us remember, various as our excursions are—that we have still set our faces towards Jerusalem—that we have a place of rest and happiness, towards which we hasten, and that the way to get there is not so much to please our hearts, as to improve them in virtue. (Vol. I, pp. 20-21)[5]

It would seem that Yorick, by Sterne's standards in the sermons, would be welcome to all the pleasures of his sentimental quest so long as he does not lose sight of the ultimate "place of rest and happiness." Most of the passages of the *Sentimental Journey* which strike a

[5]This passage was rewritten from that in Sterne's earlier Sermon XXXVII, Vol. II, pp. 258-259. In some passages the earlier version is even more Shandian: "The humoring of certain appetites, where morality is not concerned" are the means by which God sweetens life. "And a man might, with as much reason, muffle up himself against sunshine and fair weather,—and at other times expose himself naked to the inclemencies of cold and rain, as debar himself of the innocent delights of his nature, for affected reserve and melancholy."

Margaret R. B. Shaw in *Laurence Sterne: the Making of a Humorist, 1713-1762* (London: Richards Press, 1957), pp. 108-112, makes an interesting explication of Sterne's defence of joy in this lively sermon, pointing out that Sterne's concept of happiness derives ultimately from Aristotle's *Ethics,* where happiness is defined as "an activity of the soul in accordance with perfect virtue."

modern reader as maudlin have to do with his desire for tender pleasures. The two insipid stories called "Le Patisser" (*sic*) and "The Sword," which have nothing to do with the general development of the narrative, he offers as delicate tidbits for the sentimental palate—"As I have told this to please the reader," Yorick explains about the first story, "I beg he will allow me to relate another, out of its order, to please myself" (p. 148). If one postulates a benevolent passion, he will expect to find a companion appetite for that sentiment. Sterne speaks to the point in the sermons, saying about literary representations of benevolence, "I think there needs no stronger argument to prove how universally and deeply the seeds of this virtue of compassion are planted in the heart of man, than in the pleasure we take in such representations of it" (Vol. I, p. 48).

Nevertheless, to the extent that Yorick's search for pleasure turns him aside from his main goal, he is in grave danger. "The deceiver of mankind" tempts men by "making them dream of wondrous gratifications they are to feel in following their appetites" (Vol. II, p. 122).[6] Indeed benevolent acts are pleasant. They satisfy an instinct. But the same can be said of many forbidden acts. Consequently, seeking pleasure as such, while it may not be wrong, is yet acting without any moral guidance. Thus, it can compete with duty in the moral choices open to man. Virtue, as Sterne believes, may be "pleasant in the way, as well as in the end" (Vol. II, p. 133). But keeping on the proper way without being sidetracked by vicious pleasures involves serious problems.

This dilemma Sterne incorporated into his sentimental adventure story.[7] When Yorick meets a fair *fille de chambre* in a bookseller's

[6]The sentence is plagiarized from Edward Young; see Hammond, pp. 184-185.

[7]I shall concentrate in this chapter upon the Paris scenes which constitute the bulk of Vol. II. I find it necessary, however, to depart from a chronological account. For the reader who wishes to refresh his memory, here is a brief chronology of those scenes:

Friday evening: (1) Yorick meets the *fille de chambre* and walks part of the way home with her (pp. 119-124).

(2) Arriving at the hotel, he learns the police are looking for him: he is without a passport in a nation with which England is at war. His fears of the Bastille aroused by a caged bird mechanically crying, "I can't get out," Yorick plans to go the Prime Minister in the morning (pp. 125-136).

Saturday: (1) On the road to Versailles, Yorick tells the history of the bird (pp. 137-139).

(2) Unable to get an audience with the Duc de Choiseul, he meets

shop, he purposely follows her out the door, and in the tradition of Christian soliders on foreign soil, he talks to her of love. But Yorick talks as a Christian ought—he admonishes her to keep her chastity: " 'tis a little treasure to thee, and gives a better air to your face, than if it was dressed out with pearls.' Thereupon, he makes "a virtuous convention" with her: taking her purse, he drops in one of the crowns he had intended for Shakespeare, saying, "Be but as good as thou art handsome, and heaven will fill it" (pp. 120-121). Yorick thus satisfies—or attempts to satisfy—the desire for pleasure and the call of duty. He enjoys the girl's handsome face while preach-

---

a *pâtissier*, who turns out to be a former soldier, knighted for bravery, but now courageously fighting poverty (pp. 140-148).

(3) Yorick then tells the story of a nobleman who nobly recoups a lost fortune by applying himself to commerce—"The Sword" (pp. 149-151).

(4) Yorick asks help of the Comte de Bissy and has a long visit with this Anglophile. The Count obtains a passport for "Mr. Yorick, the king's jester" (pp. 152-167).

(5) Returning to the hotel, he finds the *fille de chambre* in his room. There follows a violent struggle with his passions, after which Yorick cools himself in the darkened street. There he notices a beggar who wins large sums of every woman who passes, but who avoids all men (pp. 168-177).

(6) The appearance of indiscretion involves Yorick in an argument with the hotel keeper, who wants no women in the rooms but those who will share with him the profits. Yorick tries to avenge himself by insulting a girl the man sends up, but finds he cannot be unkind (pp. 178-184).

Sunday: (1) Unable to refuse La Fleur a holiday, Yorick spends the day translating a fragment of an old page which has wandered into his room wrapped about a print of butter. The fragment tells the story of a notary and his "fume" of a wife—pointedly suggestive of Mrs. Sterne (pp. 185-196).

(2) The fragment ends before the climax of the story. Yorick sends La Fleur in search of the rest, which had left the hotel wrapped about La Fleur's bouquet and had been passed from one amorous hand to another amorous hand all over Paris. Of course, the page has been lost (pp. 197-198).

Monday—probably; the day is not specified: Again at the Opéra Comique, Yorick overhears the successful beggar; the man is making a plea to two spinsters. His secret is flattery (pp. 199-203).

Indefinite period—probably two or three weeks: Introduced into the Paris salons by the Comte de Bissy, Yorick puts to use the secret and flatters his way to popularity. But growing sick of this "vile prostitution of myself," he flies southward from Paris (pp. 204-209).

ing to her the law of God. "I never gave a girl a crown in my life which gave me half the pleasure," yet, "it was a small tribute . . . to virtue." But Yorick is on dangerous ground. When they stop to dispose of the two volumes she has purchased,

> I held the second for her whilst she put the first into her pocket; and then she held her pocket, and I put the other after it.
> 'Tis sweet to feel by what fine-spun threads our affections are drawn together. (pp. 123-124)

The most humorous blurring of Christian love and sexual love comes when Yorick tells her goodnight:

> She bid me adieu twice—I repeated it as often; and so cordial was the parting between us, that had it happened anywhere else, I'm not sure but I should have signed it with a kiss of charity, as warm and holy as an apostle's.
> But in Paris, as none kiss each other but the men—I did, what amounted to the same thing—
> I bid God bless her. (p. 124)

Thus, in the struggle between Christian duty and the desire for pleasure, Sterne reveals that close texture of what Herbert Read called "the desires of the flesh and the aspirations of the spirit."

Where, then, does one draw the line between innocent pleasure and evil? Sterne provides an answer in the sermons: "One principal reason, why God may be supposed to allow pleasure in this world, seems to be for the refreshment and recruit of our souls and bodies, which, like clocks, must be wound up at certain intervals" (*Sermons*, Vol. II, p. 264). To the degree that pleasure goes beyond this purpose it becomes evil. "Whenever we pay this tribute to our appetites, any further than is sufficient for the purposes for which it was first granted,—the action proportionably loses some share of its innocence." How is one to know when that point is reached? It is easy, thinks Sterne: "there are very few who are not casuists enough to make a right judgment in this point" (Vol. II, pp. 264-265).[8]

Yorick's casuistry upon this very point provides much of the comedy of the *Journey*. His flirtations are hardly innocent pleasures, yet Yorick treats every act of courtship except coition itself as a "recruit" of body and soul. Where women are concerned, he "would

---

[8]Sterne believed that pain and sorrow have but one use in this life: they make us consider the future life, inclining us toward more virtuous conduct. See Sermon II as well as Vol. I, p. 323, and Vol. II, p. 262.

do anything in the world either for, or with anyone, if they will but satisfy me there is no sin in it" (p. 62). And at the very height of his temptation at the time the *fille de chambre* comes to his hotel room, Yorick flatly refuses to destroy his delicious sensations, saying about the devil tempter,

> I seldom resist him at all; from a terror, that though I may conquer, I may still get a hurt in the combat—so I give up the triumph, for security; and instead of thinking to make him fly, I generally fly myself. (p. 170)

So intent is Yorick upon the thrill of his experience that his consciousness of virtuous obedience to the law of chastity becomes, not an end in itself as it would be for the "happy" man of true virtue, but another means to sensational pleasure:

> There is a sort of pleasing half guilty blush, where the blood is more in fault than the man—'tis sent impetuous from the heart, and virtue flies after it—not to call it back, but to make the sensation of it more delicious to the nerves—'tis associated. (p. 169)

Finally, at the highest pitch of the "battle," when the *fille de chambre* is *renversée* on the bed, Yorick eloquently declares that all these delicious sensations are his rightful gift from God:

> Yes—and then—Ye whose clay-cold heads and lukewarm hearts can argue down or mask your passions, tell me, what trespass is it that man should have them? or how his spirit stands answerable to the father of spirits, but for his conduct under them?
>
> If nature has so wove her web of kindness, that some threads of love and desire are entangled with the piece, must the whole web be rent in drawing them out?—Whip me such stoics, great governor of nature! said I to myself—wherever thy providence shall place me for the trials of my virtue—whatever is my danger—whatever is my situation—let me feel the movements which rise out of it, and which belong to me as a man, and if I govern them as a good one, I will trust the issues to thy justice—for thou hast made us, and not we ourselves. (p. 173)[9]

[9]This famous passage echoes another Sterne had written in Sermon XVIII, "The Levite and His Concubine." Sterne there describes the

Sterne's sermons fairly groan under the strain of an interest divided between Heaven and heaven-on-earth. It is to his credit that he saw the humor implicit in his position and exposed it in his comedy of moral sentiments.

Yorick has a second moral shortcoming which is closely related to his hedonistic bent, but distinguishable from it. He has an intellectual or philosophic fault. He cannot see in benevolence its universal reference; he is not aware how it affects the social or the cosmic order.

One can hardly doubt that the Good Samaritan of Sterne's third sermon embodies his ideal of goodness. We can see in the Samaritan qualities of benevolence quite different from the simple impulses of Yorick in the *Sentimental Journey*. "This duty of the love of our neighbor," explains Sterne, rests upon a "true bottom of philanthropy and universal kindness"; the Samaritan is an "example of universal benevolence" (Vol. I, pp. 37-38).[10] "You are not to imagine" that the Samaritan's concern for the injured man was "mechanical." Instead, "there was a settled principle of humanity and goodness which operated within him" (Vol. I, p. 45). Consequently, his care is more than momentary, and it continues even when the pitiful object is not present to his senses. The Samaritan's behavior is

> like the warm zeal of a brother, mixed with the affectionate discretion and care of a parent, who was not satisfied with taking him under his protection, and supplying his present wants, but in looking forwards for him, and taking care that his wants should be supplied when he should be gone, and no longer near to befriend him. (Vol. I, p. 48)

Sterne's point is just that goodness does *not* depend upon a spontaneous instinctive response or the pleasures it brings. The Samaritan's benevolence continues even when he is removed from its object,

---

Levite's joy in his not-quite-legal wife: "Let the torpid monk seek heaven comfortless and alone.—God speed him! For my own part, I fear I should never so find the way: let me be wise and religious—but let me be Man: wherever thy Providence places me, or whatever be the road I take to get to thee—give me some companion in my journey, be it only to remark to, How our shadows lengthen as the sun goes down;—to whom I may say, How fresh is the face of nature! How sweet the flowers of the field! How delicious are these fruits!" (Vol. I, p. 290).

[10]The disciples of Christ are similarly distinguished by "that benevolent frame of mind towards all our fellow-creatures" (Vol. II, p. 319).

and it is stable rather than momentary.[11] He is able coolly to cal-
culate a social need, desire to supply the need independently of any
sensation, and act upon this general desire. His benevolence extends
itself, thus, beyond particular objects of sense to any need of the
society he can envisage; it is in this sense a "universal benevolence."

These hints indicate, I believe, that Sterne follows in general the
moral thought of his own time. Regardless of their important differences, philosophers of many schools agreed that a truly moral decision had to be made in terms of such a universal view. Shaftesbury believed the individual must elect to support the divinely
ordained "system" of heaven and earth; but the giving in to affections—even of benevolence—which do not accomplish this goal,
he strongly castigated as capricious and destructive.[12] Hutcheson
thought the merit of a generous affection should be measured by
the degree to which it embraces society at large.[13] And David Hume
decided that the limited instincts of compassion, however winning
in themselves, were apt to be harmful unless supported by consider-

[11]Of this quality of permanence we get a hint in the scene in the glove
shop of the *Sentimental Journey*. "Anyone may do a casual act of good
nature," Yorick says to the *grisette*, "but a continuation of them shows it
is a part of the temperature" (p. 96).

[12]*Characteristics of Men, Manners, Opinions, Times*, ed. John M.
Robertson (London: Grant Richards, 1900), Vol. I, pp. 280, 299-300.

[13]*Inquiry into the Original of our Ideas of Beauty and Virtue* (London,
1738), pp. 180-181. Hutcheson's discussion of the point in *An Essay on
the Nature and Conduct of the Passions and Affections. With illustrations
on the Moral Sense* (London, 1728) describes the notion fully, pp. 29-
31: "... our public desires may be distinguished into the general calm
desire of the happiness of others, or aversion to their misery upon reflection; and the particular affections or passions of love, congratulation,
compassion, natural affection. These particular affections are found in
many tempers, where, through want of reflection, the general calm
desires are not found: Nay, the former may be opposite to the latter,
where they are found in the same temper. We obtain command over the
particular passions, principally by strengthening the general desires
through frequent reflection, and making them habitual, so as to obtain
strength superior to the particular passions.

"Again, the calm public desires may be considered as 'they either
regard the good of particular persons or societies presented to our senses;
or that of some more abstract or general community, such as a species
or system.' This latter sort we may call universal calm benevolence. Now
'tis plain, that not only particular kind passions, but even calm particular
benevolence do not always arise from, or necessarily presuppose, the
universal benevolence; both the former may be found in persons of little

ations of the needs of society at large.[14] Similarly, Bishop Butler's "general principle of benevolence" explained in his twelfth sermon, according to C. D. Broad, amounts to

> a rational calculating principle, which must be sharply distinguished from a mere impulsive sympathy with people whom we see in distress. It is the principle which makes us try to maximise the general happiness according to a rational scheme and without regard to persons. I think it would be fair to say that the ideal of the Charity Organization Society is benevolence in Butler's sense.[15]

The rational moralists, too, embrace this principle, claiming that the consideration of the whole society is a dictate of reason. The point is made by Thomas Nettleton in his anonymously published work, *Some Thoughts Concerning Virtue and Happiness* (London, 1729):

> But, as objects which are near are apt to affect us more, and those that are distant, less, than they ought; our benevolence may possibly exceed its due bounds towards some, while it is deficient towards others; so that this very best and noblest disposition may prove pernicious, if it is not directed by *right reason*; as that instead of being partial and narrow, and limited to a few, it may be entire and universal, extended in a due proportion to all *mankind*. (p. 69)[16]

A good man makes a practice of reasoning out the needs of his whole society and looks upon the need of a particular person in terms of its large effects. He acts upon these cool considerations, which are complementary to, but above and distinct from his immediate impulses of benevolence or their promised pleasures. By the moral standard of the eighteenth century, hinted at in Sterne's sermons,

---

reflection, where the latter is wanting: and the former two may be opposite to the other, where they meet together in one temper."

[14]*Enquiry*, Sec. V, Pt. II, pp. 218-232.

[15]*Five Types of Ethical Theory*, p. 61.

[16]See also John Balguy, *Letter to a Deist*, in *A Collection of Tracts Moral and Theological* (London, 1734), pp. 23-24, whose ideal is "Christian benevolence, which comprehends . . . the whole species, and spreads itself over the face of the whole earth. Instead of that partial love, those contracted affections whether for kindred, neighbors, friends or country, which both Jews and Gentiles were too apt to run into, and even make their boast of; Christianity requires us to love all without distinction, and opening our arms as wide as possible, embrace mankind with an universal good-will."

a universal reference ought to be part of Yorick's benevolence.

Yet in the *Sentimental Journey*, Yorick cannot think in these abstract terms. He is limited to his instinctive reactions to particular objects of pity. In his lack of perspective lies the import of the well-known incident of the caged starling. When Yorick learns that he may be arrested for traveling in an enemy nation without a passport, he tries to laugh off the danger: "a tower is but another word for a house you can't get out of—Mercy on the gouty!" Musing this, as he walks down the hotel passageway, he hears a childlike voice crying, I can't get out—I can't get out!" Yorick's reaction to the starling's mechanical plea is itself mechanical.

> God help thee! said I, but I'll get thee out, cost what it will; so I turned about the cage to get the door; it was twisted and double twisted so fast with wire, there was no getting it open without pulling the cage to pieces—I took both hands to it.
>
> . . . I fear, poor creature! said I, I cannot set thee at liberty— "No," said the starling—"I can't get out—I can't get out," said the starling.
>
> I vow, I never had my affections more tenderly awakened. . . .
> (p. 132)

Many critics have pointed to the story of this bird as evidence of Sterne's "insincerity" in sentimental writing. Sterne luxuriates in emotions, they say, but the starling is never set free. Instead, Yorick purchases him and gives him rather bad treatment—he passes him from hand to hand as a show. The critics are quite right that setting the bird free would have been, for Yorick, the proper moral act. They err only in assuming the story is designed as an example of morality or to give a superficial appearance of morality. The purpose of the story, I contend, is to show the working of the native, but amoral passions of benevolence. Yorick's immediate response is an attempt to free the bird (a point the critics generally overlook); if we read imaginatively, our fingers ought to ache sympathetically as Yorick tries to break that cage. Yet once the impulse has passed, the desire to free the bird is gone with it. There is no stability in Yorick's charity, nor is there any calm consideration of man's obligation to beasts or the effect of this example of cruelty on society.

The scene which follows demonstrates Yorick's inability to think abstractly about moral problems. Worried now about the Bastille, he shuts himself in his room.

I began to figure to myself the miseries of confinement. I was in the right frame for it, and so I gave full scope to my imagination.

I was going to begin with the millions of my fellow creatures born to no inheritance but slavery; but finding, however affecting the picture was, that I could not bring it near me, and that the multitude of sad groups in it did but distract me.—

—I took a single captive, and having first shut him up in his dungeon, I then looked through the twilight of his grated door to take his picture. (p. 134)

Thereafter he conjures up a striking and moving image of a particular prisoner. But he could not be affected by the general idea of slavery.

Yorick has not the benevolent temper of the Samaritan in Sermon III. He cannot be affected by abstract considerations and general ideas; as a result he has no control over his particular benevolent impulses and cannot extend his charities beyond an original impetus.[17] He may lecture to the Monk with considerable aplomb upon the

[17] I do not mean to imply that, in Sterne's view, ideal benevolence must be utilitarian, in the narrow sense of that word. For Sterne there are two universal considerations, depending upon whether he is thinking of the moral law or the motives to act upon it: these are reason (see below, Chapter V) or the acceptability of an act to God. Sterne was not interested in the welfare of society as such. "The best moral discourses," he comments, "may prove little better than a cold political lecture" unless we add to them the "arguments of religion" (Vol. II, p. 52). We distort Sterne's fiction when we look for a sociological or utilitarian approach. This misunderstanding underlies Sir Leslie Stephen's blast at Sterne as a "literary prostitute" in his *History of English Thought in the Eighteenth Century* (London: Smith, Elder, 1876), Vol. II, p. 443: "When Rousseau wept rather too freely over the sorrows of his heroine, he regarded her as a type of the woman of his time; and, therefore, was consciously aiming at a social and moral revolution. Sterne was content to weep without the slightest indication of any desire for a change. He shows no sense whatever of evils affecting the general welfare." To be sure, Sterne was not thinking of utility. But he was concerned for moral *character*, and his ideal includes an ability to think out the universal implications of an act and to allow that consideration to affect moral decisions. Henry D. Aiken makes the same point about Hume's ethic: ". . . it is a serious mistake to *identify* moral goodness, as the utilitarians maintained, with whatever conforms to the so-called greatest happiness principle. In pronouncing moral judgments, according to Hume, we do *not* look to the *consequences* of an act, but to the motives or character of him who performs it. In short, morality is mainly concerned with questions of virtuous character rather than questions of good behavior"—"Introduction" to *Hume's Moral and Political Philosophy* (New York: Hafner, 1948), p. xxxiv.

principle of charity, distinguishing between the deserts of the needy poor and those of the mendicant orders (pp. 8-9). But he hardly convinces himself. And as soon as the Monk performs a particular act of good-will, Yorick decides the Franciscan must be the epitome of virtue. Yorick's moral framework is nothing like the temper of the Good Samaritan. The Samaritan would have found a way to express his convictions about poverty in acts more significant than buying compliments from beggars; he would have been affected by the abstract idea of slavery; he would have freed the starling as soon as he could get some pliers to break the wire; he would have prevented the servant's cruelty to the post horse. But Yorick has not that kind of goodness.

Instead of trying to discipline himself to become a man of virtue, Yorick interests himself in every sensational pleasure of benevolence. In the end, his sensibility appears to be only a bagatelle, a laughable thing, much as his concern for an unhappy carriage "standing so many months unpitied" in the corner of Monsieur Dessein's coach-yard:

> —Now was I the master of this hotel, said I, laying the point of my fore-finger on Monsieur Dessein's breast, I would inevitably make a point of getting rid of this unfortunate *désobligeant*—it stands swinging reproaches at you every time you pass by it—
>
> *Mon Dieu*! said Monsieur Dessein—I have no interest—Except the interest, said I, which men of a certain turn of mind take, Monsieur Dessein, in their own sensations—I'm persuaded, to a man who feels for others as well as for himself, every rainy night, disguise it as you will, must cast a damp upon your spirits—You suffer, Monsieur Dessein, as much as the machine— (p. 21)

But Sterne knew perfectly well that those who take such an interest in their own sensations when feeling for others, have but a transitory and meritless benevolence:

> ... every looker-on has an interest in the tragedy;—but then we are apt to interest ourselves no otherwise, than merely as the incidents themselves strike our passions, without carrying the lesson further:—in a word—we realize nothing:—we sigh— we wipe away the tear,—and there ends the story of misery, and the moral with it. (*Sermons*, Vol. II, p. 8)

The most elevated consideration in Yorick's conduct is his awareness of God. But even that strikes us as undignified and "Water-
landish"[18] orthodox. He lives in fear of the God "before whose
tribunal I must one day come and give an account of this work"
(p. 18).[19] But his moral character is so rudimentary as to be laughable. His fear of punishment shows clearly when he discovers the
fille de chambre in his hotel bedroom. Yorick is searching for a paper
upon which to write a note for the girl's mistress, when he notices
that the setting sun tints her face. Yorick blushes; and recalling that
they are alone, he blushes a second time:

> I felt something at first within me which was not in strict unison
> with the lesson of virtue I had given her the night before—I
> sought five minutes for a card—I knew I had not one—I took
> up a pen—I laid it down again—my hand trembled—*the devil
> was in me.*
>
> *I know as well as any one, he is an adversary, whom if we
> resist, he will fly from us. . . .*
>
> I have nothing, my dear, said I, to write upon.—Write it, said
> she, simply, upon anything.—
>
> I was just going to cry out, Then I will write it, fair girl! upon
> thy lips.—
>
> —*If I do*, said I, *I shall perish*—so I took her by the hand,
> and led her to the door, and begged she would not forget the
> lesson I had given her. (pp. 169-170; italics mine)

But the girl is not easily sent away, and somehow they find them-

---

[18]The coinage is Sterne's—*Tristram Shandy*, p. 427. Daniel Waterland
(1683-1740) was a leader in the opposition to Latitudinarianism. He
held that virtue was defined exclusively by the fiat of God, that without
divine retribution the actions we now call virtuous would be morally in-
distinguishable from those we now call sinful or foolish. Waterland, a
notorious pluralist, held the Chancellorship of York Cathedral in the
period immediately before Sterne joined the Cathedral Chapter, though
it is unlikely he spent much time in York. See William Whewell, *Lectures
on the History of Moral Philosophy* (Cambridge: Deighton, Bell; London: Bell and Daldy, 1862), pp. 152-153.

[19]True, Sterne defined the duties of religion as having the fear of God
(Vol. II, p. 110). But he thought that such a "fear" brought peace to a
good man because it taught him "how to receive these certain vicis-
situdes of life,—the returns of good and evil, so as neither to be exalted
by the one, or overthrown by the other" (Vol. I, pp. 253-254; Vol. II,
p. 315). Yorick's fear brings no peace; he seems blind to the cosmic
order.

selves seated on the bed. She must show him the little purse she has
made for his crown. "I held it ten minutes with the back of my hand
resting upon her lap, looking sometimes at the purse—sometimes
on one side of it." The fair innocent insists upon sewing the gathers
broken out of Yorick's stock—"I foresaw it would hazard the glory
of the day; and as she passed her hand in silence across and across
my neck in the maneuver, I felt the laurels shake which fancy had
wreathed about my head" (p. 172). Eventually, Yorick manages to
fear God and keep his commandments; the girl leaves unviolated.[20]
But before he retires that night, he orders that she not be admitted
if she comes again: "This was a sacrifice . . . to . . . myself, having
resolved, after so narrow an escape, to run no more risks, but to leave
Paris, if it was possible, with all the virtue I entered it" (p. 182).

We find this forced and unwilling obedience to God's law throughout all Yorick's flirtations. Debating with himself whether he will
be unfair to Eliza if he goes to see Madame de L*** in Brussels,

> Eternal fountain of happiness! said I, kneeling down upon
> the ground—be thou my witness—and every pure spirit which
> tastes it, be my witness also, that I would not travel to Brussels,
> unless Eliza went along with me, did the road lead me towards
> heaven.
>
> In transports of this kind, the heart, in spite of the under-
> standing, will always say too much. (p. 80)

Yorick comes close, at times, to virtue, but in each instance
Sterne puts a twist on the narrative which forces us to accept his
benevolence as instinctive and particular rather than considered and
universal. For instance, when La Fleur asks for a holiday at a time
when Yorick wants his services, Yorick grants the favor upon what
appear to be highly moral grounds:

> . . . the sons and daughters of service part with liberty, but not
> with nature, in their contracts; they are flesh and blood, and

[20]Yorick has deluded himself, of course, about the innocence of the
fille de chambre. In the earlier scene with her, when they are walking
in the Paris evening, Yorick says, "I see innocence, my dear, in your
face—and foul befall the man who ever lays a snare in its way!" Her
reaction and Yorick's own reaction to hers reveals much about the girl
and about Yorick's self-deception: "The girl seemed affected some way
or other with what I said—she gave a low sigh—I found I was not im-
powered to inquire at all after it—so said nothing more till I got to the
corner of the Rue de Nevers, where we were to part" (p. 122).

have their little vanities and wishes in the midst of the house
of bondage, as well as their taskmasters. . . .

Behold!—Behold, I am thy servant—disarms me at once
of the powers of a master— (p. 187)

Yet the prefatory comment reveals that Yorick is hardly thinking
out the broad implications of his act: "But we must *feel*," he says,
"not argue in these embarrassments."

Another instance is "The Case of Conscience." The appearance
of indiscretion in the visit of the *fille de chambre* involves Yorick
in a quarrel with the hotel keeper. This unpleasant man insists upon
his own sort of discreet conduct: he will send up a girl with a
band box who sells "lace and silk stockings and ruffles, *et tout cela*,"
implying that he will close his eyes to what really happens in the
room—and share the girl's profit too. Yorick decides to permit
this scurrilous plan so that he can avenge himself. But his conscience
will hardly allow him to entertain such a thought.

Now shall I triumph over this *maître d'hôtel*, cried I—and
what then?—Then I shall let him see I know he is a dirty
fellow.—And what then?—What then!—I was too near myself
to say it was for the sake of others.—I had no good answer left
—there was more of spleen than principle in my project, and
I was sick of it before the execution. (p. 179)

When the girl arrives, she is such a pathetic creature, so anxious
to earn a penny, that poor Yorick ends by buying a pair of ruffles
and insulting no one. But at the very point when Sterne has developed
a picture of Yorick, acting with quiet moral dignity, he destroys the
illusion by revealing that, after all, his decision had been determined:
"The master of the hotel will share the profit with her—no matter—
then I have only paid as many a poor soul has *paid* before me for
an act he *could* not do, or think of."

To my mind, the most untainted of all Yorick's benevolence is
revealed in the droll story of his helping a little boy across the gutter
of a wet street—"Upon turning up his face to look at him after,
I perceived he was about forty—Never mind, said I, some good
body will do as much for me when I am ninety." If in this instance
Sterne does not openly rob his protagonist of the merit of the good
deed, he still leaves in question whether the kindness is impulsive or
made upon calm considerations: "I feel some little principles within
me," comments the clerical protagonist, "which incline me to be
merciful towards this poor blighted part of my species, who have

neither size or strength to get on in the world—I cannot bear to see one of them trod upon" (p. 110).

That Yorick finds no contentment in his hobby is made evident by the rapidity with which he gives up the quest for benevolence in favor of the affectation of it. He has been in Paris only a few days when he learns the secret of flattery from an unusual beggar. This man "of a philosophic serious . . . look" Yorick had noticed outside his hotel. He had spoken only to women, but from each had received unusually generous sums. Later, in a dark entrance to the Opéra Comique, Yorick chances to overhear the man practice his wiles upon two maiden ladies, flattering their vanity, not only about beauty and rank, but about their benevolence: "What is it but your goodness and humanity which makes your bright eyes so sweet, that they outshine the morning even in this dark passage?" Yorick has his secret—" 'twas flattery"—which, after all, has much the same effect upon the passions as genuine good-will: "Delicious essence! how refreshing art thou to nature! how strongly are all its powers and all its weaknesses on thy side! how sweetly dost thou mix with the blood, and help it through the most difficult and tortuous passages to the heart!" (p. 203). Without hesitation Yorick puts to use this mockery of his moral investigation. The Comte de Bissy, having done him one favor, introduces him into the salons of "a few people of rank," and given that start, Yorick flatters his way mightily to the top of Parisian society. Yet the new pleasure palls as quickly as the old:

> . . . 'twas a dishonest *reckoning*—I grew ashamed of it—it was the gain of a slave—every sentiment of honor revolted against it—the higher I got, the more was I forced upon my *beggarly system*—the better the *coterie*—the more children of Art—I languished for those of Nature; and one night, after a most vile prostitution of myself to half a dozen different people, I grew sick—went to bed—ordered La Fleur to get me horses in the morning to set out for Italy. (p. 209)

The gist of Yorick's hobby-horsical quest is this: the benevolence he discovers is the beginning of morality, but it is not moral enough; the reward of his charity is pleasure, but he never finds peace. Man, as Sterne sees him in the novels, is frustrated by his own enthusiastic determination to seize upon his ideal. Walter Shandy is obsessed with hypotheses, but never finds the truth; Mr. Yorick is obsessed with benevolence, but he never finds virtue. Although Yorick wants to strip naked the human heart to find what therein "to fashion my own by," the effect of his exfoliation is to discover only the anatomy of human nature. Of course, from his "humorific" point of view as narrator, Yorick is a wiser man—but that is not the subject of the *Sentimental Journey*. As a traveler to France he had mistakenly assumed that the anatomy of benevolence was the morality of God, and that made him the fool Sterne intended him to be.

Chapter IV

THE COMIC COSMOS

Laurence Sterne died twenty days after the appearance of the *Sentimental Journey*. He had been dying for eight years. Although by his own testimony, he enjoyed good health during his years as the vicar of Sutton and Stillington, he must have known since that night at Cambridge when he was awakened by a hemorrhage of the lungs "bleeding the bed full" that consumption would claim him before he had lived out a normal life. His hasty trip to France in 1762, which provided so many rich materials for the *Journey*, was a flight from death, and made famous as that by the seventh volume of *Tristram Shandy*. Yet Sterne could not reconcile himself to a life which prepares for death. "I am ill—very ill," he wrote to Elizabeth Montagu from his death bed. "Yet I feel my existence strongly, and something like revelation along with it, which tells, I shall not die— but live——and yet any other man would set his house in order—" (*Letters*, p. 416).

Sterne imparted to Yorick of the *Sentimental Journey* all the apprehensions of a man suspended between the impending need to set his house in order and the need to "exist." Yorick too is an "invalid," so "pale and sickly" that the Comte de Bissy insists upon his sitting during their interview. The image of death is scattered throughout the *Sentimental Journey*—from the opening scene in which Yorick mourns that the French king will take from his dead body even the picture of Eliza, to the last, when Yorick, weak and coughing, refuses to sleep in a drafty closet. We are never far removed from the grave of the Monk, the dead ass in the road, or the death-bed of the old man in the notary's story. We cannot mistake the image when Yorick, newly arrived in Paris, walks "gravely to the window in my dusty black coat, and looking through the glass saw all the world in yellow, blue, and green, running at the ring of pleasure. . . . Alas, poor Yorick! cried I, what art thou doing here? On the very first onset of all this glittering clatter, thou art reduced to an atom" (pp. 88-89). Yorick even identifies himself to the Comte de Bissy by opening *Hamlet* and pointing to the grave-digger's scene. "Now whether the idea of poor Yorick's skull was put out of the Count's mind, by the reality of my own, or by what magic he could drop a period of seven or eight hundred years, makes nothing in this account—'tis certain the French conceive better than they combine" (pp. 157-158). Nevertheless, the Count obtains for Yorick a passport "directed to all lieutenant governors, governors, and commandants of cities, generals of armies, justiciaries, and all officers of justice, to let Mr. Yorick, the king's jester, and his baggage, travel quietly along." Thus the English parson acquires the identity of a jester known to the world only as a skull and a memory.[1] The hero of Sterne's sentimental comedy juggles with the most serious things of life—love and desire and morality—mere baubles in his clever hands. Only when we become aware that Yorick juggles on a tightrope with death below and God above, do we begin to see the high seriousness of this humor.

This tension becomes most apparent in the few pages of the *Sentimental Journey* following Yorick's hasty exodus from Paris. The tone of the narrative rises as the journey accelerates. Impatient of indecision in his quest, Yorick takes matters firmly in hand: he *will* experience the good; he will wrest from life its secrets before his vile cough wrests life from him.

Sterne allows Yorick three final adventures. First he searches out Maria, the demented peasant girl Sterne had introduced into the ninth volume of *Tristram Shandy*, a maid of great beauty who had gone out of her mind because her marriage had been forbidden. He next happens upon a peasant family, with whom he sups and prays—the very children of nature he had hoped to find. One discovers in these scenes more references to God than in all the rest of the novel taken together. Inspired by his feelings of pity and love, Yorick reaches out for that universal reference he has not yet experienced, for a vision of the divine which will give meaning to his hobby of benevolence. But at the height of his humorous mysticism, Sterne annihilates all moral and religious ideals in a final comedy. In the trials

[1] Ben Reid, in "The Sad Hilarity of Sterne," *Virginia Quarterly Review*, XXXII (1956), 107-130, maintains "that it is not chance, not the need for a simple generic title, but the tragic sense of life that dictates the choice of Yorick for a name. Surely the nimbus that endures in our recollection of Yorick is not that he was 'a fellow of infinite jest,' 'wont to set the table in a roar,' but the fact that he *was*: the fact that we meet him as a skull, 'quite chap-fallen,' grown plaything of a foolish sententious rustic, 'knocked about the mazzard with a sexton's spade' " (p. 111).

of sharing a room with a lady in a wayside inn, Yorick reveals all his own meanness and his conventional religionism.

The seeking out of Maria is clearly a quixotic undertaking: " 'Tis going, I own, like the Knight of the Woeful Countenance, in quest of melancholy adventures." And Yorick knows ahead of time—as he had known upon arriving in France—that sentimental commerce is the key to life's secrets: "I know not how it is, but I am never so perfectly conscious of the existence of a soul within me, as when I am entangled in them" (p. 211).[2] He at last discovers Maria under a poplar "sitting with her elbow in her lap, and her head leaning on one side within her hand." Yorick sends La Fleur to arrange his supper while he talks with her. One of the most famous "Beauties of Sterne" follows:

> Her goat had been as faithless as her lover; and she had got a little dog in lieu of him, which she had kept tied by a string to her girdle; as I looked at her dog, she drew him towards her with the string—"Thou shalt not leave me, Sylvio," said she. I looked in Maria's eyes, and saw she was thinking more of her father than of her lover or her little goat; for as she uttered them the tears trickled down her cheeks.
>
> I sat down close by her; and Maria let me wipe them away as they fell with my handkerchief.—I then steeped it in my own—and then in hers—and then in mine—and then I wiped hers again— (pp. 212-213)

And—as Yorick had anticipated—the experience teaches him he has a soul: "I felt such undescribable emotions within me, as I am sure could not be accounted for from any combinations of matter and motion. I am positive I have a soul; nor can all the books with which materialists have pestered the world ever convince me of the contrary" (p. 213). But the reader has become wary of Yorick's feelings toward beautiful women; one easily sees that Yorick celebrates his soul to hide the truth about his desires:

[2]During the Calais meal, while Yorick had held out his purse, looking for someone to take it, he had said, "I felt every vessel in my frame dilate—the arteries beat all cheerily together, and every power which sustained life, performed it with so little friction, that 'twould have confounded the most *physical précieuse* in France: with all her materialism, she could scarce have called me a machine" (p. 4). Yet this was the very moment when Yorick becomes mechanical to an extreme in his reactions to the Monk.

Maria, though not tall, was nevertheless of the first order of
fine forms—affliction had touched her looks with something that
was scarce earthly—still she was feminine—and so much was
there about her of all that the heart wishes, or the eye looks for
in woman, that could the traces be ever worn out of her brain,
and those of Eliza's out of mine, she should *not only eat of
my bread and drink of my own cup*, but Maria should lay in my
bosom, and be unto me as a daughter. (p. 217)

I am sure Yorick feels genuine pity for this attractive lunatic; his
paraphrase of Nathan's parable of the poor man's love for his lamb
(II *Samuel*, 12:1-4) is not just fortuitous. Yet we cannot escape the
suspicion that Sterne knew perfectly well how the Biblical phrase
"lay in his bosom" acquired quite another meaning in this new context. That Yorick's feelings ought to be taken as a revelation of his
immortal soul, the reader will doubt.

The image of Maria remains with Yorick as he travels on through
Bourbonnais, unfitting him for "so joyous a riot of the affections" as
the festive grape harvesting promises. At length, while thinking of
her, the surface of his moral inquiries seems to break, revealing an
insight which Yorick takes to be profoundly metaphysical—a recog-
nition of divine altruistic sympathy, a God whose essence is benevolence:

I had got almost to Lyons before I was able to cast a shade
across her—

—Dear sensibility! source inexhausted of all that's precious
in our joys, or costly in our sorrows! thou chainest thy martyr
down upon his bed of straw—and 'tis thou who lifts him up to
Heaven—eternal fountain of our feelings!—'tis here I trace thee
—and this is thy divinity which stirs within me——not that, in
some sad and sickening moments, *"my soul shrinks back upon
herself, and startles at destruction"*—mere pomp of words!—but
that I feel some generous joys and generous cares beyond myself—All comes from thee, great, great Sensorium of the world!
which vibrates, if a hair of our heads but falls upon the ground,
in the remotest desert of thy creation.—Touched with thee,
Eugenius draws my curtain when I languish—hears my tale of
symptoms, and blames the weather for the disorders of his
nerves. Thou givest a portion of it sometimes to the roughest
peasant who traverses the bleakest mountains—he finds the
lacerated lamb of another's flock—This moment I behold him

learing with his head against his crook, with piteous inclination looking down upon it—Oh! had I come one moment sooner!—it bleeds to death—his gentle heart bleeds with it—

Peace to thee, generous swain!—I see thou walkest off with anguish—but thy joys shall balance it—for happy is thy cottage—and happy is the sharer of it—and happy are the lambs which sport about you. (pp. 218-219)

In this apostrophe to sensibility, Yorick extends his prejudices about natural benevolence to their furthest reaches. Sensibility he sees as cosmic, for it lifts its martyr to Heaven. It has eternality and divinity—"eternal fountain of our feelings—'tis here I trace thee—and this is thy divinity which stirs within me." But the choice of a new word, *sensibility*, hardly alters the fact that Yorick refers to particular impulses of benevolence, for they are "generous joys and generous cares beyond myself" such as those felt by Eugenius (Sterne's rakish friend, John Hall-Stevenson) when his friend is ill, such as those felt by the rough peasant for the wounded lamb of another's flock.

Yet surely this metaphysics was laughable to Laurence Sterne. The humor is apparent in Yorick's claiming salvation and divinity for his feelings toward a good-looking paranoiac in the words of Joseph Addison's pompous Cato. In Act V, Scene I, the noble Roman is found,

> *solus, sitting in a thoughtful posture; in his hand Plato's Book on the Immortality of the Soul [the Phaedo?]. A drawn sword on the table by him.*

> Cato: It must be so—Plato, thou reasonest well!—
> Else whence this pleasing hope, this fond desire,
> This longing after immortality?
> Or whence this secret dread, and inward horror,
> Of falling into nought? Why shrinks the soul
> Back on herself, and startles at destruction?
> 'Tis the divinity that stirs within us;
> 'Tis heaven itself, that points out an hereafter,
> And intimates eternity to man.

Of course, as Yorick reads them, the lines come out somewhat altered to suit his predisposition.

... eternal fountain of our feelings!—'tis here I trace thee—

and this is thy divinity which stirs within me——not that, in some sad and sickening moments, *"my soul shrinks back upon herself, and startles at destruction"*—mere pomp of words!—but that I feel some generous joys and generous cares beyond myself.

If Cato had been reading the Phaedo, Yorick surely had not. Yorick's notion of immortality is hardly a temper which becomes divine as it is purged of all emotions; Yorick's sort of immortality is inverted Platonism, the glorification of emotions—so long as they are tender and sympatheic.

More than this: the essential nature of God, as Yorick sees Him, is his benevolent compassion—"great, great Sensorium of the world, which vibrates, if a hair of our heads but falls upon the ground, in the remotest desert of thy creation." The words *Sensorium* and *vibrates* are striking; by suggesting the vibration theory of the nerves, they imply that God responds emotionally to every event of the universe—a God of feeling and sympathy.[3] The notion of a God

[3]Originally the word *sensorium* had meant the center of the nervous system; later it came to mean "mind." In *Tristram Shandy* Sterne used the word in each of these senses, respectively, on page 149 and page 638. The meaning narrowed in various discussions of epistemological dualism to designate the physical system which can know the outside world; see, for example, David Harley, *Observations on Man* (London, 1749) I, i, l, Prop. III; or the anonymous associationist work, probably by James Long, *An Enquiry into the Origin of the Human Appetites and Affections* (Lincoln, 1747), p. 60. Sterne's use of the word in the apostrophe suggests, however, the controversy which arose over a passage in Newton's *Opticks*. Newton has referred to space as the sensorium of God: "... does it not appear from phenomena that there is a Being incorporeal, living, intelligent, omnipresent, who in infinite space, as it were in his sensory, sees the things themselves intimately, and thoroughly perceives them, and comprehends them wholly by their immediate presence to himself: of which things the images only carried through the organs of sense into our little sensoriums, are there seen and beheld by that which in us perceives and thinks." In another passage, Newton speaks of God "who being in all places, is able by his will to move the bodies within his boundless uniform sensorium"—quoted by H. G. Alexander in his "Introduction" to *The Leibniz-Clarke Correspondence* (New York: Philosophical Library, 1956), pp. xv-xvi. The passage was attacked by Leibniz as an implication that God needed sense organs. Samuel Clarke answered by arguing that Newton had meant the opposite—God, through his being in space, had no need of sensations. Joseph Addison supported Clarke, and incidentally popularized the word, in *Spectator* No. 565 (July 9, 1714). Yorick's use of the word in the apostrophe, however, suggests

of Love is part and parcel of Christian orthodoxy, but it is only part. The position which distinguishes Christianity from so many other religions is that the God of Love is synthesized with the God of Justice and Power. In his sermons, Sterne consistently takes this Christian stand. If God can be thought of as having "kind and benevolent affections of his nature," Sterne is sure to add that these are not like the "sensitive and corporal part" of man and are linked with God's "rectitude," that is, his reason (Vol. I, p. 113). Sermon XXXIV, "Trust in God," has some lines suggestive of Yorick's apostrophe: Sterne speaks of God, "who sees all those conflicts under which thou laborest,—who knows thy necessities afar off,—and puts all thy tears into his bottle." But in the same sentence, he describes God as both "infinitely kind and powerful" (Vol. II, pp. 217-218). Sterne speaks in this sermon of God "in whose hands are the issues of life and death, and without whose knowledge and permission we know that not a hair of our heads can fall to the ground" (Vol. II, p. 215)—a line strongly suggestive of the God of power described in *Matthew*, 10:30, "But the very hairs of your head are all numbered." In the apostrophe of the *Sentimental Journey*, Yorick conceives God as passively and benevolently concerned for falling hairs. The infatuated Yorick is not to be taken as the spokesman for the philosophy of Laurence Sterne.

Nor can we doubt that Yorick's mystic sensibility is the logical extreme of his original prejudiced opinion about the morality of particular benevolence. The apostrophe forms the complement, in a positive form, of an idea Yorick had put negatively in his early attacks upon Smelfungus (Tobias Smolett) and Mundungus (Samuel Sharp). Their rejection of pity and sympathy, as Yorick had seen it in the earlier statement, set them apart, not only from society, but from the divine:

> Peace be to them! if it is to be found; but Heaven itself, was it possible to get there with such tempers, would want objects to give it—every gentle spirit would come flying upon the wings of Love to hail their arrival.—Nothing would the souls of Smelfungus and Mundungus hear of, but fresh anthems of joy, fresh raptures of love, and fresh congratulations of their common felicity—I heartily pity them: they have brought up no faculties for this work; and was the happiest mansion in heaven to be

---

the notion of which Leibniz had accused Newton—that God has sensation.

allotted to Smelfungus and Mundungus, they would be so far from being happy, that the souls of Smelfungus and Mundungus would do penance there to all eternity. (p. 52)[4]

If egoistic withdrawal fits one only for penance, Heaven must be reserved for people of sensibility—such as Yorick. And that is what Yorick thinks he has learned mystically through his lovely vision.

[4]In writing this passage, Sterne may have amused himself in a private joke; for he describes Smollet and Sharp through an idea and image he had used in the sermons while quoting John Norris, who in turn appears to have taken the image from John Tillotson. These Latitudinarians, giving their respective versions of Plato's metapsychology in the *Phaedo* (Steph. 80B-84D), had described this same worldly malcontent in the heavenly mansions. Tillotson wrote, "... heaven consists in such things as a wicked man hath no gust and relish for. ... If a man of an envious and malicious, of a peevish and passionate temper, were admitted into the mansions of the blessed, he would not only be unhappy himself, but would disturb the quiet of others, and raise storms even in those calm regions"— Sermon VIII, "Of the Happiness of a Heavenly Conversation," *Works*, ed. Thomas Birch (London, 1752), Vol. I, p. 76. John Norris expresses the idea, borrowing the image of the heavenly mansions: "... should an impure soul be afforded a mansion in heaven, she would be so far from being happy in it, that she would do *penance* there to all eternity. For besides that a sensualized soul would carry such appetites with her thither for which she could find no suitable object, which would be a constant torment; those that she *does* find there would be so disproportionate, that they would rather vex and upbraid, than satisfy her indigence"— sixth discourse of *Practical Discourses upon the Beatitudes* . . . , edition of 1694, Vol. I, pp. 166-167 (see also Hammond, p. 142). Sterne quotes the passage in his Sermon XXIX, "Our Conversation in Heaven": "The consideration of this had led some writers so far as to say, with some degree of irreverence in the expression,—that it was not in the power of God to make a wicked man happy, if the soul was separated from the body, with all its vicious habits and inclinations unreformed;—which thought a very able divine in our church has pursued so far, as to de-clare his belief,——that could the happiest mansion in heaven be supposed to be allotted to a gross and polluted spirit, it would be so far from being happy in it, that it would do penance there to all eternity;— by which he meant, it would carry such appetites along with it, for which there could be found no suitable objects.—A sufficient cause of constant torment;—for those that it found there . . . would rather vex and up-braid it, than satisfy its wants" (Vol. II, p. 142). By this circuitous route, the Platonism of Tillotson becomes the hobby-horsical philosophy of Yorick; and a "voluptuous epicure," as Sterne describes the unspiritual man, who "knows of no other happiness in this world, but what arises from good eating and drinking;—such a one, in the apostle's language, whose God is his belly" (Vol. II, pp. 140-141) becomes Tobias Smollett!

In the following scene, Yorick is exposed to the most simple and complete good-will of the entire *Journey*. He is brought to a little farm house in a small vineyard, where "an old grey-headed man and his wife, with five or six sons and son-in-laws and their several wives, and a joyous genealogy out of 'em" are sitting down to bread and wine in "a feast of love."

> The old man rose up to meet me, and with a respectful cordiality would have me sit down at the table; my heart was sat down the moment I entered the room; so I sat down at once like a son of the family; and to invest myself in the character as speedily as I could, I instantly borrowed the old man's knife, and taking up the loaf cut myself a hearty luncheon; and as I did it I saw a testimony in every eye, not only of an honest welcome, but of a welcome mixed with thanks that I had not seemed to doubt it.

> Was it this; or tell me, Nature, what else it was that made this morsel so sweet—and to what magic I owe it, that the draught I took of their flagon was so delicious with it, that they remain upon my palate to this hour? (pp. 221-222)

There is no mockery in Sterne's handling of the scene. These homey, generous people have that *politesse de coeur* for which Yorick has been searching. And they have religion. Their unusual danced prayer gives Yorick an opportunity to associate his own idiosyncrasy with their "cheerful and contented minds."

> It was not till the middle of the second dance, when, from some pauses in the movement wherein they all seemed to look up, I fancied I could distinguish an elevation of spirit different from that which is the cause or the effect of simple jollity—In a word, I thought I beheld *Religion* mixing in the dance—but as I had never seen her so engaged, I should have looked upon it now, as one of the illusions of an imagination which is eternally misleading me, had not the old man, as soon as the dance ended, said, that this was their constant way; and that all his life long he had made it a rule, after supper was over, to call out his family to dance and rejoice; believing, he said, that a cheerful and contented mind was the best sort of thanks to heaven that an illiterate peasant could pay—
> ——Or a learned prelate either, said I. (pp. 223-224)

Sterne, who had written a strikingly similar description of a thanksgiving dance in his sermon, "The Prodigal Son,"[5] surely admired a willingness to "serve the Lord with gladness" and to "come before his presence with singing," as we are told to do in the hundredth Psalm. The only question here is whether or not Yorick, in the brief interval between the arch-benevolism of the apostrophe to sensibility and the debased religionism of the final story—"The Case of Delicacy"—learns or can learn anything from these simple people.

The final incident of the *Sentimental Journey* Sterne worked up from an anecdote told him by an acquaintance, John Craufurd. It is a light, off-color story in the manner of the Medieval fabliau. But, playful as it is, it reveals at length the truth of Yorick's moral and religious quest. There we discover that the benevolence he prizes is not forthcoming when Yorick's health and comfort are in jeopardy, that his God is a perfectly conventional law-giving, law-enforcing deity.

Soon after Yorick leaves the peasant family he is caught up in the events at that "little decent kind of an inn by the roadside" to which he is forced when a large stone blocks the road. No sooner is he established in the one guest room than a *voiture* arrives bearing a handsome Piedmontese lady of about thirty and her "brisk and lively" Lyonnais serving-maid, whose journey has been interrupted by the same stone.

> As there was no other bed-chamber in the house, the hostess, without much nicety, led them into mine, telling them, as she ushered them in, that there was nobody in it but an English gentleman—that there were two good beds in it, and a closet within the room which held another . . . and she durst say, the gentleman would do anything to accommodate matters. (pp. 226-227)

The bed in the closet, however, hardly alleviates the difficulty; the

---

[5] "When the affections so kindly break loose, Joy is another name for Religion.

"We look up as we taste it: the cold Stoic without, when he hears the dancing and music, may ask sullenly . . . what it means? and refuse to enter: but the humane and compassionate all fly impetuously to the banquet. . . . Gentle spirits, light up the pavilion with a sacred fire; and parental love and filial piety, lead in the mask with riot and wild festivity! —Was it not for this that God gave man music to strike upon the kindly passions; that Nature taught the feet to dance to its movements, and, as chief governess of the feast, poured forth wine into the goblet, to crown it with gladness?" (Vol. I, p. 327).

glass is gone from its window and the shutter is half dismantled—"so it reduced the case in course to this alternative—that the lady should sacrifice her health to her feelings, and take up the closet herself, and abandon the bed next mine to her maid, or that the girl should take the closet, &c. &c." The decision is finally reached that the maid must suffer the cold of the closet, while Yorick and the lady must suffer the trials of twin beds snugly recessed behind the chimney and so closely placed as to allow only a small wicker chair between them.

In such a situation, Yorick's sensibility hardly evidences the divine in him. He remains as delicately sensitive as ever, but his keen perceptions lead him only to assert his own desires at the expense of others:

> The lady had scarce warmed herself five minutes at the fire, before she began to turn her head back, and give a look at the beds; and the oftener she cast her eyes that way, the more they returned perplexed—I felt for her—and for myself; for in a few minutes, what by her looks, and the case itself, I found myself as much embarrassed as it was possible the lady could be herself. (p. 227)

Here is no generous sympathy, but an acute observation of the enemy. Yorick feels for her—and himself. When she peeps into the closet, he but coughs the louder to announce he will not be imposed upon. Furthermore, sensibility prevents Yorick and the Piedmontese from solving their problem. The narrow space between the beds is "oppressive to us," their recessed position "no way favorable to the nicety of our sensations." Ironically, in "The Case of Delicacy," delicacy hinders the frank facing of a moral problem. "The obstacle of the stone in the road . . . was but a pebble to what lay in our ways now. . . . it did not lessen the weight which hung upon our spirits, that we were both too delicate to communicate what we felt to each other upon the occasion." But a few bottles of Burgundy in the lady's *voiture* are able to overcome their embarrassment and to allow the pair to feel "inspired with a strength of mind sufficient to talk, at least, without reserve upon our situation." As the novel begins in mild intoxication upon Burgundy sufficient to inspire self-satisfying and false benevolence, so it ends in mild intoxication upon Burgundy sufficient to overcome sensibility.

The truth about Yorick's attitude toward God begins to show in the "treaty of peace" which the pair draw up with their wine-loosened tongues.

We turned it every way, and debated and considered it in all kinds of lights in the course of a two hours negotiation; at the end of which the articles were settled finally betwixt us, and stipulated for in form and manner of a treaty of peace—and, I believe with as much religion and good faith on both sides, as any treaty which has yet had the honor of being handed down to posterity. (p. 230)

Considering the purpose of the treaty, one cannot doubt the *double-entendre* in the word *posterity*. Religion and carnality begin to converge. They are brought closer together in the three articles of the treaty. Article I settles who is to take which bed and that the flimsy, transparent curtains of the lady's are to be pinned closed. Article II stipulates that Yorick shall sleep in his black silk breeches (which from the first pages have symbolized his priesthood). Article III keeps Yorick's God before us:

3rdly. It was insisted upon, and stipulated for by the lady, that after Monsieur was got to bed, and the candle and fire extinguished, that Monsieur should not speak one single word the whole night.

Granted; provided Monsieur's saying his prayers might not be deemed an infraction of the treaty. (p. 231)

Upon sensibility and religion the final joke turns. A wordless understanding between the pair is the cause of their sleeplessness, and an address to the deity the cause of their quarrel. After lying quietly until one o'clock,

when Nature and patience both wearing out—O my God! said I—

—You have broke the treaty, Monsieur, said the lady, who had no more slept than myself.—I begged a thousand pardons, but insisted it was no more than an ejaculation—she maintained 'twas an entire infraction of the treaty—I maintained it was provided for in the clause of the third article. (p. 232)

As the argument grows warm and the corking pins begin to fall out of the curtain, the maid sneaks through the total darkness to put herself between her mistress and the Englishman, so that when Yorick stretches out his hand by way of (punning) "asseveration," he catches the "*fille de chambre's* END OF VOL. II."

In Yorick's apostrophe, "dear sensibility" is the key to Heaven;

in "The Case of Delicacy," sensibility is an obstacle to frankness and good-will. In the apostrophe, the God of Love offers universal sympathy; in the scene at the inn, the God of Justice is the chance advent of a bawdy joke. Sterne leaves Yorick's conflicting moral and religious sentiments as they are—in perpetual, paradoxical suspension. The synthesis of these opposites, the simple human generosity of the peasant family and their immediate doxology, the hobby-riding Yorick cannot make his own. For him, benevolence remains a natural, lovely characteristic of man, and chastity remains the extra-natural command of God. The final incident discovers Yorick obeying that command, but enjoying the titillation of his amorous desires, a man of courtesy and sensibility, but anxious after his own comfort. He still has not found the joy of understanding or the peace of goodness.

Chapter V

THE HEAD AND THE HEART

In the existing portion of the *Sentimental Journey*, Yorick is left hanging between hobby-horsical benevolence and reluctant obedience. But neither of these extreme sentiments constitute what Laurence Sterne considered the moral ideal, for at bottom Sterne was a rationalist in his ethic. He understood and admired the emotions of the heart, but he knew that reason ought to command those "movements." In his travel novel, he drew no picture of the calm, good man, with reason in firm control; he chose instead to present the fundamental comic fact which perpetually amused him—the heart can and does trick the head. For all that, however, Sterne's humor implies an ideal of moral reason.

My opinion will seem odd to those who regard Sterne primarily as a sentimental novelist. The scenes of pathos in the *Sentimental Journey* are so brilliant that for many casual readers they outshine the moral comedy. The episodes of the Monk, the old soldier, the peasant family, and Maria have claimed the tears and loyalties of countless numbers. For such readers, the fleeting moments of sympathy in which Sterne's characters give themselves to others without reserve, transcend all Sterne's clowning to express an authentic moral and aesthetic good. The moment of love, though it be no more than a moment, Yorick sometimes invests with the highest value by regarding it as having no end beyond itself:

I pity the man who can travel from *Dan* to *Beersheba*, and cry, 'Tis all barren—And so it is; and so is all the world to him who will not cultivate the fruits it offers. I declare, said I, clapping my hands cheerily together, that was I in a desert, I would find wherewith in it to call forth my affections—If I could not do better, I would fasten them upon some sweet myrtle, or seek some melancholy cypress to connect myself to—I would court their shade, and greet them kindly for their protection—I would cut my name upon them, and swear they were the loveliest trees throughout the desert: if their leaves withered, I would

103

teach myself to mourn, and when they rejoiced, I would rejoice along with them. (p. 50)

Indeed, Sterne did think that benevolence was a beautiful, satisfying thing which had its own rewards quite aside from its place in the moral character.[1] But if that were his only view, he would be the treasurer of a very moderate value. Pity and sympathy and love are to be found in the *Sentimental Journey*, but we must not lift them out of context to make of Sterne a votary of the heart and nothing else.

Sterne's sentimentalism cannot explain his comedy. A humorist, as Jean Paul Richter pointed out, has the broadest possible perspective. He writes about man's greatness and smallness, but sees both in a totality which makes "everything equal and nothing before the infinite."[2] To a humorist, the winning sympathetic affections, the beautiful union of spirits still bound by flesh, have no higher value than the fleshy lusts themselves.

Those who have little respect for Sterne as a historic personality will think it ridiculous to claim for him such a noble vision. For Swift or Johnson, yes. These were great humanists with enlarged understandings. I have no doubt these men were more powerful personalities than the Rev. Mr. Laurence Sterne; most certainly they were more admirable than he in their personal conduct. But for all that, Sterne had a moral and religious perspective much like theirs, for he too was an eighteenth-century rationalist.[3]

But a rationalist "believes in" the heart as well as the reason. The

[1]Sterne never forgot in his sermons that salvation was everyone's goal. Still, "the very thing which made life desirable" was benevolence (Vol. I, p. 116). Again in Sermon XLI, "Look into private life,—behold how good and pleasant a thing it is to live together in unity;—it is like the precious ointment poured upon the head of Aaron, that run down to his skirts;—importing, that this balm of life is felt and enjoyed, not only by governors of kingdoms, but is derived down to the lowest rank of life, and tasted in the most private recesses;—all, from the king to the peasant, are refreshed with its blessings, without which we can find no comfort in anything this world can give.—It is this blessing gives every one to sit quietly under his vine, and reap the fruits of his labor and industry (Vol. II, p. 317).

[2]*Vorschule der Aesthetik*, in *Sämtliche Werke* (Weimar: Hermann Bönlaus Nachfolger, 1935), Abt. I, Bd. 11, Ch. 32.

[3]Since this study was written, I have come to the conclusion that Sterne's rationalism, indeed his entire ethic, owes more to Locke's *Essay Concerning Human Understanding* than this chapter indicates. See my article, "The Sermon in *Tristram Shandy*," *ELH*, XXXI (1964), 395-417.

Latitudinarians, Samuel Clarke, Richard Price, all thought the passions were necessary and useful. So, for that matter, did Alexander Pope:

> On life's vast ocean diversely we sail,
> Reason the card, but Passion is the gale.
> —*Essay on Man*, II, iii

Sterne's instinct psychology, his religious eudaemonism, his notion of an ideally benevolent temper, do not rule out his acceptance of reason as the key principle in ethics. Sterne's salient sentimental values can be understood and accepted by those who admire Sterne the humorist once they understand his ideal of a personality harmonized by reason. Only a writer who believed that reason ought to rule the heart could discover Sterne's fundamental comic fact—that the heart can and does trick the head. An anonymous critic in the *Times Literary Supplement* (April 9, 1949, p. 232) commented,

> Sterne, poised between the Age of Reason and the Age of Feeling, is one of the least sentimental writers, for he never confused his heart with his head. . . . It was with pleasure that he noticed the incongruities of his heart, how at one moment he could dream of transforming the world by benevolence, and at the next moment be planning to enclose Stillington Common from the poor.
>
> . . . Reality for Sterne was neither reason nor feeling, but the opposition of the two.

The *general* fault of Yorick in the *Sentimental Journey* is this: he fails to govern himself. There is nothing wrong in his having strong affections, but he is wrong in easily giving himself up to their rule. He is right to obey the commands of God, but wrong in capitulating to them unthinkingly. Sterne believed man should have more autonomy than has Yorick, which amounts to saying he should rule himself through reason. God has endowed man with "liberty and free-will;—he has set life and death, good and evil, before him; . . . he has given him faculties to find out what will be the consequences of either way of acting, and then left him to take which course his reason and direction shall point out" (*Sermons*, Vol. II, p. 357). This attitude, which Sterne shares with all Christian rationalists, assumes that reason and will are virtually synonymous: ". . . not only religion but even reason itself, must necessarily imply a freedom of choice; and all the beings in the world, which have it, are created free to stand or free to fall" (Vol. II, p. 198).

Like other moralists who put their faith in reason, Sterne assumes that reason has the power to organize the affections and shape the temper of an agent. Some ruling passion may come to dominate the emotional disposition through the force of habit, but reason can step in at any point to override or break or make a habit. "When the edge of appetite has been worn down, and the heat of pursuit pretty well over,—and reason and judgment have got possession of their empire—they seldom fail of bringing the lost sheep back to his fold" (Vol. I, pp. 316-317). There are, of course, many lost sheep. That sensations or passions or hobby-horses do escape the scrutiny of reason is Sterne's observation of life. "The judgments of the more disinterested and impartial of us," he wrote in Sermon XIX,

> receive no small tincture from our affections: we generally consult them in all doubtful points, and it happens well if the matter in question is not almost settled before the arbitrator [reason] is called into the debate; but in the more flagrant instances, where the passions govern the whole man, 'tis melancholy to see the office to which reason, the great prerogative of his nature, is reduced; serving the lower appetites in the dishonest drudgery of finding out arguments to justify the present pursuit. (Vol. I, pp. 313-314)

Pope's version of a trite metaphor in *Spectator* No. 408 (Wednesday, June 18, 1712) is as good an expression as any of Sterne's ordinary doctrine:

> . . . the passions . . . are to the mind as the winds to a ship, they only can move it, and they too often destroy it; if fair and gentle they guide it into the harbor; if contrary and furious they overset it in the waves: In the same manner is the mind assisted or endangered by the passions; reason must then take the place of pilot, and can never fail of securing her charge if she be not wanting to herself: the strength of the passions will never be accepted as an excuse for complying with them; they were designed for subjection, and if a man suffers them to get the upper hand, he then betrays the liberty of his own soul.

Could we, writes Sterne, "learn to weigh the causes, and compare the consequences of things, and to exercise the reason, which God has put into us for the government and direction of our lives,—there would be some hopes" (Vol. I, p. 225). For a rationalist, reason always can and always ought to rule the heart. In his fiction, Sterne chose to emphasize that, in fact, it seldom does so.[4]

A comic novelist has no intention of destroying his humorous effects by giving away the joke. Sterne does not make a direct statement that Yorick's mechanical benevolence misses the moral mark. But he does give a hint early in the book: he describes Yorick's selfish responses to the Monk as automatic reflexes. Yorick, recognizing the mechanical nature of his reaction, wistfully yearns to lose himself in this inner force and thereby escape his responsibilities; but he knows he cannot:

> I had scarce uttered these words, when a poor monk of the order of St. Francis came into the room to beg something for his convent. No man cares to have his virtues the sport of contingencies—or one man may be generous, as another is puissant—*sed non, quo ad hanc*—or be it as it may—for there is no regular reasoning upon the ebbs and flows of our humors; they may depend upon the same causes, for ought I know, which influence the tides themselves—'twould oft be no discredit to us to suppose it was so: I'm sure at least for myself, that in many a case I should be more highly satisfied, to have it said by the

[4]Perhaps Sterne reflects an attitude pointed out by A. O. Lovejoy: the eighteenth-century rationalist tended to keep his claims to reason at a minimum— " 'Pride' in Eighteenth-Century Thought," *Essays in the History of Ideas* (Baltimore: Johns Hopkins Press, 1948), pp. 62-68. To be sure, Sterne thinks reason is sufficient for man's moral needs; but at the same time, "That in many dark and abstract questions of mere speculation, we should err,——is not strange: we live among mysteries and riddles, and almost everything which comes in our way, in one light or other, may be said to baffle our understandings" (Vol. I, p. 312). This common idea in the sermons (see also Vol. I, p. 297; Vol. II, pp. 367-368), Sterne used as a minor theme of *Tristram Shandy*: "But mark, madam, we live amongst riddles and mysteries—and the most obvious things, which come in our way, have dark sides, which the quickest sight cannot penetrate into; and even the clearest and most exalted understandings amongst us find ourselves puzzled and at a loss in almost every cranny of nature's works" (p. 293). "We live in a world beset on all sides with mysteries and riddles" (p. 625). It seems likely that Sterne included these pronouncements as complements to Walter Shandy's intellectual fumbling. But an awareness of the limitations of reason is not to be taken as a capitulation to passion. Sterne could never have subscribed to Hume's famous dictum, "Reason is, and ought only to be the slave of the passions"—*Treatise of Human Nature*, ed. L. A. Selby-Bigge (Oxford: Clarendon, 1896), p. 415.

world, "I had had an affair with the moon, in which there was neither sin nor shame," than have it pass altogether as my own act and deed, wherein there was so much of both.

—But be this as it may. The moment I cast my eyes upon him, I was predetermined not to give him a single *sou.* (p. 5)

The statement is difficult to follow, but with some care its meaning is clear enough: Sterne will not permit his protagonist to excuse any response as "an affair with the moon," that is, as a mechanical action which cannot be controlled. Sterne calls upon us, in this manner, to judge Yorick's character, and surely he means us to condemn Yorick whenever he allows his passions to "determine" him, be they selfish or benevolent.

Sterne thinks that reason ought to *sanction* every moral decision. The revealed word of God is holy and perfect, but one ought not to give himself even to that law in slavish, unquestioning obedience. For him, "faith" is a "rational assent of the understanding to truths which are established by indisputable authority" (Vol. II, p. 284). Sterne dislikes any talk about the Spirit of God in ourselves unless we mean the critical attempt to make the gospel "consistent with itself" and "consistent with reason and common sense" (Vol. II, p. 271). Sterne cannot tolerate "enthusiastic" religions, such as the Quakers, whose members resign themselves to a spirit descending mystically and felt emotionally. No, man can meet God only in the rational; we are raised "from nothing, to the dignity of rational creatures, made, with respect to our reason and understanding, after His own most perfect image" (Vol. II, p. 339).[5] God would not destroy this dignity by manifesting himself otherwise than through reason:

As expressly as we are told to pray for the inspiration of God's spirit, there are no boundaries fixed, nor can any be ever marked to distinguish them from the efforts and determinations of our own reason. ... there never was a Christian of a cool head and sound judgment, that, in any instance of a change of life, would

[5]See also Sermon X: man is "fashioned after the image of his Creator with respect to reason and the great faculties of the mind" (Vol. I, p. 162). In Sermon XIX, Sterne argues that if man misuses his reason, the fault is not with the faculty of judgment, for that "would reflect dishonor upon God; as if he had made and sent men into the world on purpose to play the fool. His all-bountiful hand made his [man's] judgment,, like his heart, upright" (Vol. I, pp. 312-313).

presume to say, which part of his reformation was owing to divine help,—or which to the operations of his own mind. (Vol. II, pp. 70-71)

It seems obvious that Yorick's acceptance of divine commands, especially that of chastity, has none of the dignity belonging to a man who uses reason to assure himself of the validity of the law. He is the slave of fear, which wells up in him thoughtlessly and suddenly.

In short, Yorick is at fault when his goals are dictated by his own emotional nature, for in such cases he allows himself to be a measure of his own moral conduct. That is what Sterne remonstrates against in "The Abuses of Conscience Considered": the moral ideal lies outside the moral agent.

> ... your conscience is not a law;—no—God and reason made the law, and has placed conscience within you to determine,— not like an *Asiatic Cadi*, according to the ebbs and flows of his own passions; but like a *British judge* in this land of liberty, who makes no new law,——but faithfully declares that glorious law which he finds already written. (Vol. II, p. 117)

Herbert Read, citing this passage, maintains that "Sterne's genius is really to be reckoned on the side of the classical forces in literature" because he believed all action must be tested against an objective moral law.[6] I feel certain Read has touched upon the major significance of Sterne's rationalism—the moral law is a truth having absolute and objective existence, like Plato's ideal forms. Personal autonomy consists of measuring one's conduct against these absolute laws; virtue is choosing to keep them; happiness is knowing they have been kept.

Sterne's rationalism is much like that of the Cambridge Platonists and their eighteenth-century followers, Clarke and his group, and Price. The moral law, these men thought, can be discovered *a priori* by reason alone, much as mathematical truths are found. The law, in fact, amounts to the duty of living by truth; Sterne's phrase is typical—"the unchangeable obligations of justice and truth" (Vol. II, p. 109). These obligatory truths are logical *relations* between man and man or between man and God; hence, they are eternal and

[6]*Collected Essays in Literary Criticism* (London: Faber and Faber, 1938), p. 260. Another interesting defense of Sterne's rationalism in this and other sermons can be found in Chapter VII of Margaret R. B. Shaw's *Laurence Sterne: the Making of a Humorist, 1713-1762*, pp. 90-100.

immutable.' God indeed demands obedience, but he does so only of

⁷The relationships among "things" (beings—either actual or potential)
consitute "eternal fitness." Because this "fitness" is a *relationship* and
not in itself a created thing, it is distinct from God's *will,* that attribute
of God which creates, as well as from His creatures. However, because
God foresees the relationships which will exist among things after they
are created, "eternal fitness" is a guide to his will. Many rationalists re-
peat the doctrine:

Samuel Clarke, *A Discourse Concerning the Being and Attributes of
God,* in *Works* (London, 1738), Vol. II, p. 575: "The same reasons,
(*viz.* the aforementioned necessary and eternal different relations which
different things bear one to another; and the consequent fitness or unfitness of the application of different things, or different relations one to
another, unavoidably arising from that difference of the things themselves;) these very same reasons, I say, which always and necessarily
do determine the will of God, as hath been before shown; ought also
constantly to determine the will of all subordinate intelligent beings."

Arthur Ashley Sykes, in his anonymously published *True Foundations
of Natural and Reveal'd Religion* . . . (London, 1730), p. 18: "Now as
the rectitude of God consists in following the fitness of things, so the
rectitude of all intelligent beings consists in the same thing. God does
not follow them, because they are suited to his convenience or interests,
nor because they are founded upon any law or command, but because
there is an agreement or fitness in the relations themselves."

John Balguy, *Letter to a Deist,* in *A Collection of Tracts, Moral and
Theological* . . . (London, 1734), p. 6: "God has no superior to prescribe
laws to him, and yet is eternally bound by rectitude of own nature [sic];
that is, the rules of right reason. These are so many laws to him, which
he perpetually and inviolably observes: they strictly and formally oblige
him; nor can the obligation be ever dissolved." Also see *The Foundation
of Moral Goodness* in Balguy's *Collection,* pp. 68-69: "Though we are
certainly obliged to do whatever appears to be the will of God, merely
because it is his will, and in consequence of that right which he has to
prescribe laws to us; yet our obligation to act conformably to reason is
even superior to this, because the divine Will itself is certainly subject
to the original law or rule of action."

William Adams, Master of Trinity College, Cambridge, *The Nature
and Obligation of Virtue* (London, 1754), p. 22: ". . . the laws of God
himself are not therefore righteous, merely because they are commanded, but are therefore commanded, because they are antecedently
and in their own nature righteous. Reason and right are the eternal rule
of action by which the will of God himself is directed."

Richard Price, *A Review of the Principal Questions in Morals,* first
published 1757, ed. D. Daiches Raphael (Oxford: Clarendon, 1948), pp.
85-87: ". . . something there certainly is which we must allow not to be
dependent on the will of God. For instance; this will itself; his own existence; his eternity and immensity; the difference between power and

such absolute laws. And so for Sterne, the "weightier matters of the law" are "of eternal and unchangeable obligation" (Vol. I, p. 105). Consequently, reason alone can show men their duty. The moral part of the ancient Jewish law, Sterne says, was "a piece of intelligence they did not stand in want of," for men always have had reason enough to discover it and wisdom enough to put it to practice "without Moses' assistance" (Vol. I, pp. 337-338).[8] A crime which is not recognized by human law, such as the murder of a patient by a quack physician, is still recognized as criminal because of "the law of right" (Vol. II, p. 239). In fact, the reason all cultures detest murder is that they all know "the law of nature" (Vol. II, p. 229). The moral and religious failures of man, whether in a pre- or post-Christian society, have never been "want of light," for the "law written in their hearts, was clear and express enough for any reasonable creature" (Vol. II, p. 83).[9]

Although benevolence may have a special claim upon the emotional temper of a good man, it too must be sanctioned by reason. Benevolence is good only because it fulfills the eternal law known to reason. In the "Vindication of Human Nature," Sterne explains how the instinctive charity of youth is "founded" in his nature by God "as a provisional security to make him social." But benevolence is more than this: it is a "reason in nature," although to a youth " 'tis reason . . . yet undiscovered" (Vol. I, p. 118). Yorick's impulses of

---

impotence, wisdom and folly, truth and falsehood, existence and non-existence." ". . . Hence we see clearly, that to conceive of truth as depending on God's will, is to conceive of his intelligence and knowledge as depending on his will. And is it possible, that any one man can think this as reasonable, as, on the contrary, to conceive of his *will* (which from the nature of it, *requires something* to guide and determine it) as dependent on and regulated by his *understanding*?—What can be more preposterous, than to make the Deity nothing but will; and to exalt this on the ruins of all his attributes?"

[8]In a like manner, Sterne thinks the Romans could have known the essentials of religion before the coming of St. Paul. "That there was one supreme Being who made this world, and who ought to be worshiped by his creatures, is the foundation of all religion, and so obvious a truth in nature,—that reason, as the Apostle acknowledges [*Romans*, 1:19-22], was always able to discover it" (Vol. II, p. 84).

[9]Sterne does not deny the lessons of experience, but he does think those of pure reason are the more important: when he is explaining how we learn about the insufficiency of the pleasures gained by satisfying appetites, he says, "we find by experience . . . it is so, and by reason that, it always must be so" (Vol. I, p. 17).

pity and charity are like those of a youth. He stands in marked contrast to the Good Samaritan of Sermon III, who reasoned fully and carefully before he acted compassionately (Vol. I, pp. 46-48), whose actions fulfill "the law" (Vol. I, p. 51).

Yorick's moral groping lacks the universal reference known to reason. When he attends to the word of God, he hardly does so in the spirit Sterne thought fit—"Look—What is written in the law of God? —How readest thou?—Consult calm reason, and the unchangeable obligations of justice and truth" (Vol. II, p. 109). Yorick ought to have seen his conduct as a concrete expression of a universal, eternal relationship among men which is implicit in the very nature of social intercourse. Had he been able to make such a reference, he would have found peace:

> . . . whoever discharges the duty thus———with a view to scripture, which is the rule in this case———and to reason, which is the applier of this rule in all cases . . . will lay the foundation of his peace and comfort where it ought to lie———that is, within himself—in the testimony of a good conscience, and the joyful expectation that, having done his most to examine his own works here, God will accept them hereafter through the merits of Christ. (Vol. I, p. 237)

The similarity of Sterne's moral thought to that of the Age of Reason[10] has been obscured by those qualities of his fiction which we associate with the romantic movement. His local color, his delight in unique personalities, his love of insignificant lore, his fascination with the odd, and his deep involvement in the sentiments of the heart seem typical of the early nineteenth century. I think Sterne did have a romantic "streak" in his disposition which manifested itself in his moral thinking as well as other ways. It constantly teased him to put his faith in the heart. An early letter of assured authenticity

---

[10]One of the finest "pre-romantic" religious poets, William Cowper, recognized the natural religion in Sterne's sermons and rejected them on that count: ". . . though I admire Sterne as a man of genius, I can never admire him as a preacher. For to say the least of him, he mistakes the weapons of his warfare, and fights not with the sword of the Spirit for which only he was ordained a minister of the Gospel, but with that wisdom which shone with as effectual a light before our Savior came as since, and which therefore cannot be the wisdom which He came to reveal to us"—letter to Joseph Hill, April 3, 1766, in *Correspondence of William Cowper*, ed. Thomas Wright (London: Hodder and Stoughton, 1904), Vol. I, 65.

hints at the attitude,[11] and shortly before his death, in a post-script to Mrs. James, he allowed himself to adopt the hobby-horsical ethic and even the wording of Yorick in the *Sentimental Journey* (p. 156): speaking of the novel, he wrote, "I told you my design in it was to teach us to love the world and our fellow creatures better than we do—so it runs most upon those gentler passions and affections, which aid so much to it" (*Letters*, p. 401). But an artist is apt to include every facet of his personality in his work. The crucial matter is not whether one can find a romantic attitude in the *Journey*, but what the book itself says about the attitude; and the narrator says explicitly, "I write not to apologize for the weaknesses of my heart in this tour,—but to give an account of them" (p. 25).

Yorick's thinking is vastly removed from that of Rousseau's Savoyard Vicar, who, I feel, typifies the romantic spirit. That clergyman's notion or moral authority is diametrically opposed to Sterne's ideal of rational conscience. "I need only consult myself with regard to what I wish to do," says the Savoyard Vicar; "what I feel to be right is right, what I feel to be wrong is wrong; conscience is the best casuist." And this conscience is distinct from reason: "Too often does reason deceive us; we have only too good a right to doubt her; but conscience never deceives us; she is the true guide of man; it is to the soul what instinct is to the body; he who obeys his conscience is following nature and he need not fear that he will go astray." [12] But for Sterne, virtue is never sanctioned by a sensation or feeling or moral sense; it is sanctioned only by reason. When Sterne's characters (or he himself) forget this ideal, they lose their autonomy and become the objects of his laughter.

[11]"The kindest affections," he wrote to Elizabeth Lumley before she became his wife, "will have room to shoot and expand in our retirement, and produce such fruit, as madness, and envy, and ambition have always killed in the bud. . . . We will build, and we will plant, in our own way— simplicity shall not be tortured by art—we will learn of nature how to live—she shall be our alchemist, to mingle all the good life into one salubrious draught" (*Letters*, p. 16). The best-known example of Sterne's romantic spirit, the so-called *Journal to Eliza*, is discussed in the appendix to this study.

[12]*Émile*, trans. Barbara Foxley (Everyman's Library edition; London: J. M. Dent; New York: E. P. Dutton, 1911), pp. 249-250. See also p. 253: "Although all our ideas come from without, the feelings by which they are weighed are within us, and it is by these feelings alone that we perceive fitness or unfitness of things in relation to ourselves, which leads us to seek or shun these things."

Ultimately, I suppose, the aim of a rationalist, even a rational fictionist, is to show those who have wandered how they can return to the influence of reason. But if the rationalist is also a humorist, as is Sterne, his method must be oblique. Sterne concentrates upon the comic deficiencies of man, allowing an occasional glimpse of a good man, such as the old soldier at the Opéra Comique, or dropping here and there a hint of his rational ethic. Consequently, the "uncritical critic" is apt to assume that the weaknesses of Tristram and Yorick express Sterne's sense of values. Sidney Lee, in his *Dictionary of National Biography* article on Sterne, maintained that "His deficiency in self-control induced a condition of moral apathy, and was the cause alike of the indecency and of the sentimentality which abounded in 'Tristram Shandy' and the 'Sentimental Journey.' " And Wilbur Cross wrote,

> Sterne was ludicrously weak in the reasoning faculty and in that poise of character which comes from it. Locke was the only philosopher whom he could understand; all others were charlatans who poured forth words without meaning. His sermons, always graceful and sometimes entertaining, display no logic, with the possible exception of one. . . . 'Reason,' Sterne once said, 'is half of it sense,' and he thereby described himself. (Cross, p. 548)

This is, to say the least, ill considered. Tristram's humorous speculations about how men are the dupes of their physical constitutions is taken to be a confession by Laurence Sterne—and, as Margaret R.B. Shaw has pointed out, taken illogically. Sterne could hardly have made such a confession unless he had an understanding of how men can rise above their senses. The passage Cross quotes is in Volume VII of *Tristram Shandy*. Bishop Hall, Tristram comments, being "very corpulent," regards motion as torture and rest as heavenly. Tristram, however, prefers motion over rest because he is so very thin. Neither, Sterne implies, is apt to be right. Truer judges would be the Pythagoreans, with their ability of " *'getting out of the body, in order to think well.'* No man thinks right whilst he is in it; blinded as he must be, with his congenial humors, and drawn differently aside, as the bishop and myself have been." Tristram is expressing Socrates' notion in the *Phaedo* that "every pleasure or pain has a sort of rivet with which it fastens the soul to the body and pins it down and makes it corporeal, accepting as true whatever the body certifies" (Steph. 83A-84D). Like Socrates, Tristram knows that only reason, free of all sensations, can know the truth about heaven. For ordinary men, however, like himself, "REASON is, half of it, SENSE; and the measure of heaven itself is but the measure of our present appetites and concoctions" (pp. 493-494). Such a statement could have been made only by a rationalist.

Virtually all of Sterne's critics (Herbert Read notably excepted) have ignored the device he chose for stating his moral position. Knowing how impossible it would be to fabricate, in a novel, some perfect character who might serve as the measure of virtue, Sterne had Corporal Trim read aloud his best moral sermon, "The Abuses of Conscience Considered." We can hardly doubt that Sterne regarded this discourse as his major moral and religious statement. It appeared first as a pamphlet in 1750, again in the first installment of *Tristram Shandy* (Vol. II, Ch. 17), and for a third time as Sermon XII, Vol. IV, of *The Sermons of Mr. Yorick*, 1766. The theme of the sermon is particularly appropriate to Sterne's humor, for it deals with the manner in which the passions trick the reason—when reason is not supported by religion.

> To have the fear of God before our eyes; and, in our mutual dealings with each other, to govern our actions by the eternal measures of right and wrong:—the first of these will comprehend the duties of religion: the second those of morality; which are so inseparably connected together, that you cannot divide these two *Tables*, even in imagination (though the attempt is often made in practice), without breaking and mutually destroying them both. (Vol. II, p. 110)

The point about religion setting the fear of God before our eyes, we can pass over quickly since it is ground we have already covered in this study. Sterne is here stating in a different way the ideas about happiness he had talked about in Sermon I: the general principle of happiness (as distinct from the "pleasures" of gratified appetite) will cause us to accept mistakenly worldly pleasure as the final goal unless we heed God's revelation of Heaven and Hell.

More germane to our present discussion is the point about reason, which judges according to "eternal measures of right and wrong," but which may be tricked by passion. Conscience, the act of judging one's own conduct, is described in the sermon as a court. Presiding over the court—at least part of the time—is Reason. In the dock stands the accused—moral action. The advocates who stand beside the accused

are Self-love and Little-interests.[13] At the back of the courtroom are
some noisy spectators who would like to be called to witness—
Favor and Affection. Last of all there is a sly character without any
bailiwick at all who keeps sneaking around the bench—he is Passion.
When the proper judge, Reason, is distracted, Passion manages to
slip into the judgment seat, and while he is there he gives a verdict of
innocent to any action that may be on trial. But when Reason is in
his rightful place, he judges accurately, pronouncing some actions
innocent and some guilty. The result of this confusion is clear enough
in the allegory—the individual dares not trust his conscience when
it approves his action, for Passion may have brought in the verdict
unjustly. Only when an action is condemned can one be certain Reason was the judge. Consequently, thinks Sterne, the rational conscience needs the support of religion. A quiet conscience by itself is
no assurance of virtue.

The statement makes quite clear that Sterne's characters are not to
be taken as expressing his moral ideal just because they look upon
themselves as decent. When a man is most self-satisfied, he is in grave
moral danger. The rule is especially applicable to Yorick in the
Sentimental Journey, who is aware of his conscience only when he
has made the most gross infractions of the moral law—his harsh
words to the Monk or his intention to be cruel to the girl sent to his
room by the *maître d'hôtel*. But when his affections rule, he is complacent. In the case of sexual desire, he is usually brought up sharply
by the remembrance of Hell, but when his sympathies are in play,
he never becomes self-critical.

Sterne's doctrine that passions and desires often escape the con-
demnation of moral reason results in a fiction so very "modern" that
many critics today speak of Sterne as a "psychological novelist." Psychological, Sterne's novels certainly are, in the sense that they offer
keen, instructive insights into the workings of the soul. But if we
mean by the word a clinically dispassionate contemplation of the
personality, *psychological* will not describe Sterne's fiction, for to the
roots Sterne was a moralist.

One is more apt to confuse than enlighten Sterne's fiction if he
attempts to explain it in the terms and theories of Sigmund Freud.
It may well be that Sterne reflects that *Zeitgeist* described by Lionel

---

[13]*Cf. Sentimental Journey*, p. 10: Yorick, trying to escape the judgment
of his conscience when he is unkind to the Monk, says, "I would have
given twenty *livres* for an advocate."

Trilling in his essay on Freud in *The Liberal Imagination* (New York, 1950)—that widespread fascination with the "dark" side of the mind which culminated in the psychoanalytic theory of the unconscious. Nevertheless, the differences between Sterne's psychological ethic and Freud's psychological analysis are, I believe, more instructive than their similarities.[14]

Sterne differs from Freud in two important ways. He thinks the goals of life are determined by reason and religion, not by the pleasure principle or the passions; but because he is confident man can achieve his goals, he concludes that the passions confuse and frustrate the reason, not that passions are hidden from consciousness.

Freud thinks that the mind has no necessary moral dimension at all. He is, in fact, contemptuous of ethics. The command to love our neighbors as ourselves he regards as "impossible to fulfil; such an enormous inflation of love can only lower its value and not get rid of the difficulty." What is more, " 'Natural' ethics, as it is called, has nothing to offer here beyond the narcissistic satisfaction of being able to think oneself better than others." [15] His distaste for orthodox religion is no less obvious: it is "so patently infantile, so foreign to reality that to anyone with a friendly attitude to humanity it is painful to think that the great majority of mortals will never be able to rise above this view of life." The purpose of life is not given by religion or philosophy. "What decides the purpose of life is simply the programme of the pleasure principle." [16] To be sure, as Lionel Trilling points out, Freud hoped to bring this principle under the regimen of reason. Most of *Civilization and Its Discontents* undertakes to study the manner in which the individual, guided by practical reason, gives up some of his private desires in order to cooperate with society. Nevertheless, Freud's hedonism underlies all:

> In the developmental process of the individual, the programme of the pleasure principle, which consists in finding the satisfaction of happiness, is retained as the main aim. Integration in, or adaptation to, a human community appears as a scarcely avoidable condition which must be fulfilled before this aim of happiness

[14]Although I do not agree with him, I find the Freudian interpretation of Sterne made by A. R. Towers the best recent comment in that vein: "Sterne's Cock and Bull Story," *ELH*, XXIV (1957), pp. 12-29.

[15]*Civilization and Its Discontents*, in *Works*, ed. and trans. James Strachey, *et al.* (London: Hogarth, 1961), Vol. XXI, p. 104.

[16]*Ibid.*, pp. 74-76.

can be achieved. If it could be done without that condition, it would perhaps be preferable.[17]

For Sterne such doctrines would have seemed anathemas. The goals of life for him were never to be found in man's emotional nature, and never in the pleasure principle. Man's purposes are known to reason and religion, as I have tried to show. His notion of reason operating in the conscience is neither romantic nor Freudian. A concept much closer to Sterne's can be found by looking back, rather than forward—to Robert Burton's *Anatomy of Melancholy*. The "rational soul," says Burton,

> is divided into two chief parts, differing in office only, not in essence; the understanding, which is the rational power apprehending; the will, which is the rational power moving: to which two all the other rational powers are subject and reduced.
>
> *Synteresis*, or the purer part of the conscience, is an innate habit, and doth signify a conversation of the knowledge of the law of God and Nature, to know good or evil. And (as our Divines hold) it is rather in the understanding than in the will. This makes the major proposition in a practic syllogism. The *dictamen rationis* is that which doth admonish us to do good or evil, and is the minor in the syllogism. The conscience is that which approves good or evil, justifying or condemning our actions, and is the conclusion of the syllogism.[18]

In their own ways, both Burton and Sterne are sound psychologists, and they are both radically moralists. Reason provides a means for gauging one's life, at every step of the way, according to the "law of God and Nature." But more than this—the very possession of reason entails the responsiblility to judge one's self morally. If it

[17]*Ibid.*, p. 140. One might think from the title that Freud had altered his views in *Beyond the Pleasure Principle*. In that work he describes numerous psychological conditions in which the individual must act from motives other than an immediate desire for pleasure. But in the final chapter, he insists that "to bind the instinctual impulses" and "to replace the primary process prevailing in them by the secondary process" is an exchange which "does not imply the suspension of the pleasure principle. On the contrary, the transformation occurs on *behalf* of the pleasure principle; the binding is a preparatory act which introduces and assures the dominance of the pleasure principle"—*Ibid.*, Vol. XVIII, p. 62.

[18]*Anatomy of Melancholy*, ed. Floyd Dell and Paul Jorden-Smith (New York: Tudor, 1948), pp. 144-146.

will take advantage of them, reason has two unobstructed views: it can see the objective moral truth, the law of God and Nature; it can regard the subjective truth, the real motives for one's actions. The comparing of the two is the exercise of conscience.

The rational theory of ethics lies at the very heart of Sterne's comedy. Within the minds of his characters the true motives of any one action are usually at variance with their conscious representation. Sterne thus describes a simple human fact he found exceedingly laughable. For Sigmund Freud the same fact spelled the doom of mankind. Freud's jolting innovation was not the theory that man is possessed of unconscious thought processes, for many people had arrived at that conclusion before (see Lancelot Law Whyte, *The Unconscious Before Freud*, New York, 1960). Freud's impact came from his dreadfully pessimistic conviction that the conscious ego will not be *able* in normal life to discover the unconscious memories or desires. Sterne's theory of reason places him at an opposite pole: he is very firm upon the point that motives of any sort—thoughts, appetites, passions, all the evidence for the court of conscience—*can* be scrutinized at will. If in daily life most men fail to see their own motives, the difficulty lies not with some insurmountable psychological barrier, but their own moral laziness. In Sterne's view, the only thing tending to remain hidden in the mind is sinfulness. Most people delay or distort their self-judgment, pushing aside unflattering thoughts, in what seemed to Sterne a never ending comedy of moral evasion.

Sterne makes a strong and explicit argument that one can know any of his own thoughts or motives *if he will but look for them*. This is a major theme of "The Abuses of Conscience Considered," and the central point of "Self-Knowledge," and "Self-Examination" (Sermons IV and XIV). Man does indeed deceive himself; his self-love flatters him and tempts him to disregard motives he dislikes (Vol. I, pp. 57, 229; Vol. II, pp. 61, 214). But once a person decides to judge his conduct, he has no problem discovering his own secret thoughts and desires. He will know them if he will "give himself leisure to reflect and trace back to their first springs" (Vol. I, p. 231). All he need do is "search his actions with the same critical exactness and same piercing curiosity, we are wont to sit in judgment upon others" (Vol. I, p. 236). The process is no more than "turning his eyes inward upon himself, and taking notice of the chain of his own thoughts and desires" (Vol. I, p. 54). Sterne's idea of self-knowledge is surely a very ancient one. Burton, for instance, merely assumes it in the *Anatomy of Melancholy*, without making any argument for it (p. 540). John Locke, however, made an explicit argument for the doctrine, and probably Sterne's emphasis upon self-knowledge reflects his interests in Locke. But whatever challenge led Sterne to speak of the concept so often and at such length, his purpose is clear—he wants his reader to know that no one can escape responsibility for his conduct.[19]

If we want to express Sterne's ethical psychology in Freudian terms, we must say that for him the mind is only "ego." Natural instincts hardly constitute what Freud thought of as the "id," since they are but thinly veiled in a sort of "pre-conscious" state and easily perceived at will. Nor do I find a suggestion of those infantile memories which hide themselves in the "id" only to crop up later as "com-

[19]In his *Philosophical Incursions into English Literature* (Cambridge University Press, 1946), pp. 88-89, John Laird is the first to offer the opinion that Sterne's notion of self-knowledge derives from Locke's *Essay*, II, i, 9, which Laird quotes. He then goes on, however, to make a criticism of Sterne which does justice to neither Locke nor Sterne. About "The Abuses of Conscience Considered," he says, "It begins by asserting that a man *must* be privy to his own thoughts and cannot be mistaken about them. Then it goes on to say that although the thing must be so, it isn't so if the man be sinful, prejudiced in his own favor, a casuist or the like. . . . Plainly if a man *must* have an infallible acquaintance with his own mind, heart and motives nothing can disturb that infallibility. . . ." There is a verbal difficulty here which Sterne acknowledged in Sermon IV when he spoke of the doctrine as a "seeming paradox" (Vol. I, p. 54). When Sterne talked about complete self-knowledge, he was speaking within the framework of Lockean epistemology; when he talked about our failures to use this knowledge, he was speaking as a moralist. Professor Laird makes it seem that Locke and Sterne had a ridiculous notion that every item of thought is at all times in the forefront of the mind. The intent of both men was to say only that what is in the immediate consciousness depends upon the will. The sentence in the *Essay* just before that which Laird quotes shows that, in Locke's view, people may or may not pay attention to, or make themselves aware of, what is in their minds. Speaking of children, Locke says, "Men's business in them is to acquaint themselves with what is to be found without; and so growing up in a constant attention to outward sensations, *seldom make any considerable reflection on what passes within them*, till they come to be of riper years; and *some scarce ever at all*" (II, i, 8; italics mine)—edition of Alexander Campbell Fraser (Oxford: Clarendon, 1894), Vol. I, p. 127. Clearly, Locke's doctrine of self-awareness which Sterne accepted does not guarantee that one *will* always know what he *can* know. It means, rather, that if one wishes to scrutinize his motives and thoughts, he can do so successfully. The theme is important also in Sterne's Sermons XVIII, XIX, XVII.

plexes." And Sterne's notion of a rational conscience looking inward to motives and outward to eternal laws can hardly suggest Freud's concept of a socially conditioned authority principle called the "super-ego."

It is quite true, however, that Yorick in the *Sentimental Journey* refuses to acknowledge obvious facts about himself, "rationalizes" his immoral desires, and tries to talk down his reason. When he wishes to invite Madame de L*** to travel with him, his conscience pricks him. But Yorick manages to avoid the moral issue by claiming that these moral feelings are really only so many dirty little passions:

> Every dirty passion, and bad propensity in my nature, took alarm, as I stated the proposition—It will oblige you to have a third horse, said Avarice, which will put twenty *livres* out of your pocket—You know not who she is, said Caution—or what scrapes the affair may draw you into, whispered Cowardice—
>
> —Depend upon it, Yorick! said Discretion, 'twill be said you went off with a mistress, and came by assignation to Calais for that purpose—
>
> —You can never after, cried Hypocrisy aloud, show your face in the world—or rise, quoth Meanness, in the church—or be anything in it, said Pride, but a lousy prebendary.
>
> But 'tis a civil thing, said I—and as I generally act from the first impulse, and therefore seldom listen to these cabals, which serve no purpose that I know of, but to encompass the heart with adamant—I turned instantly about to the lady——
>
> But she had glided off unperceived. . . . (pp. 37-38)

All of this is nonsense, of course, the psychological pot calling the psychological kettle black. Yorick has a sexual urge which he knows he ought to control, but which he wants to disguise so that he can permit its continuance. His "dream censor" operates, not in the Freudian way of masking desire as a symbolic image, but by making the rational seem irrational, the moral immoral. Still, his actions are culpable, and he could have known the truth simply by "turning his eyes inward." When he had first hired La Fleur, Yorick had agreed to give him a small sum for buying clothes. In Paris the servant appears one day in "a bright, clean, good scarlet coat and a pair of breeches of the same," allowing Yorick to congratulate himself upon his generosity. But,

> They were not a crown worse, he said, for the wearing—I wished him hanged for telling me—they looked so fresh, that *though*

I knew the thing could not be done, yet I would rather have im-
posed upon my fancy with thinking I had bought them new for
the fellow, than that they had come out of the Rue de Friperie.
(p. 185; italics mine)

Yorick's motives, sexuality or vanity, as the case may be, are not
deeply hidden. This sort of fiction is aptly described as "psychological," but not as "Freudian."

Yorick wants to "impose" upon his "fancy," that is, he wants
fancy to do the work of tricking reason. If we search Sterne's writings
for a principle of irrationality, we find only fancy or imagination.
Thus in Sermon I, he repeatedly says that we are led to mistake
transient pleasures for true happiness because the "imagination is
caught by every glittering appearance that flatters this expectation"
(Vol. I, pp. 10-11, 12, 13). In the "house of pleasure" in Sermon II,
he finds "in those loose and unguarded moments the imagination is
not always at command—in spite of reason and reflection, it will
forcibly carry him sometimes whither he would not" (Vol. I, pp.
26-27). Imagination is at fault in man's foolish pursuit of riches
(Vol. II, p. 27), in the levity of certain religions (Vol. II, p. 352),
in the delusion that retribution is far off (Vol. II, p. 206). The
enthusiasts' doctrine that the Holy Spirit is felt mystically, Sterne attacks as a "visionary notion of a heated imagination" (Vol. II, p.
285).[20] Sterne carried over the notion into the *Sentimental Journey*.
It is an important element in Yorick's temptation to make advances
to Madame de L***:

I had not yet seen her face—'twas not material; for the draw-
ing was instantly set about, and, long before we had got to the
door of the *remise, Fancy* had finished the whole head, and
pleased herself as much with its fitting her goddess, as if she had
dived into the Tiber for it—but thou art a seduced, and a seducing slut; and albeit thou cheatest us seven times a day with thy
pictures and images, yet with so many charms dost thou do it,
and thou deckest out thy pictures in the shapes of so many angles
of light, 'tis a shame to break with thee. (p. 27)

Little wonder Yorick condemns that "imagination which is eternally
misleading me" (p. 224).

We must make, at this point, a qualification. Although Sterne

[20]For other attacks upon the imagination of the enthusiasts, see Sermons XIV, XXV, XXXVII, and XXXVIII.

frequently thinks of imagination as a sort of anti-reason, it is a creative principle and as such has its constructive uses.[21] A rationalist understands that reason-as-will has limits; that is why the development of a benevolent *temper*, a disposition to respond immediately in a moral manner, is requisite to goodness. When reason does show itself to be weak, then "one passion is only to be combatted by another" (*Letters*, pp. 76, 79). To effect this healthful warfare, Sterne calls up the imagination. Yorick, in the *Journey*, feels free to lose himself in a sweet, refreshing reverie any time that "evils press sore upon me, and there is no retreat from them in this world."

> *Surely this is not walking in a vain shadow—nor does a man disquiet himself* in vain *by it*—he oftener does so in trusting the issue of his commotions to reason only.—I can safely say for myself, I was never able to conquer any one single bad sensation in my heart so decisively, as by beating up as fast as I could for some kindly and gentle sensation, to fight it upon its own ground. (pp. 159-160)

Ernest A. Baker read the passage as a disavowal of reason in favor of imagination.[22] I feel certain, however, that Sterne did not intend a denial of reason. He could have discovered the doctrine he describes in Burton's *Anatomy* (p. 477) or in numerous Latitudinarian tracts. The seventeenth- and eighteenth-century rationalists were too perceptive of human psychology to think that any one "faculty" of mind could operate effectively in isolation. The character of goodness demands a coordination of the whole personality. Yet the coordinator and judge in this internal organization must be reason.

The heart indeed tricks the head, but the head has the rightful authority. That was the ethical and psychological theory which gave form to Sterne's comic consciousness. The conflict of head and heart within Yorick provides the self-doubt and anxiety and, in a broad

[21]It is, for instance, a principle of art. Jean Baptiste Suard reported that Sterne ascribed his own creative ability "to one of those delicate organizations in which predominates the sacred informing principle of the soul, that immortal flame which nourishes life and devours it at the same time, and which exalts and varies, in sudden and unexpected ways, all sensations." This faculty, Sterne is reported to have said, "we call imagination or sensibility, according as it expresses itself, under the pen of a writer, in depicting scenes or in portraying the passions" (Cross, pp. 301-302).

[22]*History of the English Novel*, Vol. IV (London: H. F. and G. Witherby, 1930), 260-261.

and true sense, the *morality* of the *Sentimental Journey*. The abuses of conscience Sterne found on every hand, and not least within himself. Lovers of Sterne's moral comedy should remember his last letter, written from the deathbed three weeks after the appearance of his sentimental comic novel. "If I die," he begged of his dearest friend, Mrs. James, "forget the follies which you so often condemned —which my heart, not my head betrayed me into" (*Letters*, p. 419). There was no doubt, the head ought to rule the heart; it was Sterne's earliest and last conviction.

CONCLUSION

Henry Fielding, in the introduction to Book X of *Tom Jones*, wrote a manifesto of the novel which demarcates it from that older form of prose fiction, the romance. Since people of perfect virtue or perfect vice were not to be met in real life, he admonished the reader "not to condemn a character as a bad one, because it is not perfectly a good one." In this way Fielding announced the first law of the novel: man must be represented naturalistically rather than schematically. Representations of perfectly good or evil people, he went on to explain, have no real moral impact. If they affect a reader at all, they make him despair of his own shortcomings, or of the degradation of the race. However,

> if there be enough of goodness in a character to engage the admiration and affection of a well-disposed mind, though there should appear some of those little blemishes, *quas humana parum cavit natura*, they will raise our compassion rather than our abhorrence. Indeed, nothing can be of more moral use than the imperfections which are seen in examples of this kind; since such form a kind of surprise, more apt to affect and dwell upon our minds, than the faults of very vicious and wicked persons.

Thus Fielding announced what I would call the second law of the novel: avoiding all preaching, a writer must stimulate our contemplation of common moral problems.

Sterne followed these laws carefully, but, it may be, unconsciously. He wrote a sermon on Herod's ruling passion, but he brought no Herods into his fiction. We find in his novels only the "bad" Dr. Slop, who has a protected place by the Shandy hearth as everybody's favorite goat, contrasted to the good Uncle Toby, whose benevolence is marred by a military madness and a "smoke-jack" of a brain. Sterne created no characters perfect in virtue or vice. He chose instead to write about people who are odd, who are out of temper, who have mismanaged their ethical economies, who are not as good as they would like to be.

Morality and religion were integral to Sterne's thought. In his

novels they shaped his shrewd observations of life. Neither a buffoon
nor a literary prankster, Sterne took a moral stand in his fiction
which differed hardly at all from that of his sermons. The only
change was a subtle shift from clerical optimism to humorous pessi-
mism. To his parishioners, he had held out a cheerful hope for
salvation; when he turned to writing the histories of Tristram and
Yorick, he offered the reader an amusing picture of man forlornly
inadequate to his own ideals.

In terms of eighteenth-century ethics, *Tristram Shandy* is the more
"sentimental" of Sterne's two books, for it deals more directly with
emotional tempers which are threatened by certain passions. Sterne
writes about man when he "gives himself up to the government of a
ruling passion,——or, in other words, when his HOBBY-HORSE grows
head-strong" (p. 93). The comic foible amounts to a ruling passion
which, in Sterne's psychology, can dominate the moral character.[1]
An innocent little obsession can keep the character off his moral
balance. Walter Shandy is the least successful of Sterne's major
figures just because he gives in too readily to his weakness for
theories. He will spend years working on his *Tristra-paedia*, his
treatise on the education of his child, while the boy grows up willy-
nilly. Consequently, for all the interesting involutions of his personality, he does not deeply engage us; he lacks the moral tension
in Sterne's greater comedy. But Uncle Toby engrosses us—a good
and pious man whose benevolence and religion reign precariously
because they are constantly besieged by magnificent, if miniature
armies. When he sits with his corporal on the bowling green, talking
of Tom's widow and marriage and warfare, he starts to explain
patronizingly how the loss of Wynendale by the Count de la Motte
precipitated the losses of Lisle and Ghent and Bruges—when Trim
interrupts:

[1]Sterne himself assumed that the foible amounts to a ruling passion.
A physician had written Sterne, calling him a coward for satirizing the
recently dead Dr. Richard Mead in the person of Dr. Kunastrokius
(*Tristram Shandy*, p. 13). Sterne replied, "I have not cut up Doctor
Kunastrokius at all—I have just scratched him—and that scarce skin-
deep.—I do him first all honor—speak of Kunastrokius as a great man—
(be he who he will) and then most distantly hint at *a droll foible in his
character.* . . . In the same page (without imputation of cowardice) I have
said as much of a man twice his wisdom—and that is Solomon, of whom
I have made the same remark 'That they were both great men—and like
all mortal men *had each their ruling passion*'" (*Letters*, p. 89; italics
mine).

———Why therefore, may not battles, an' please your honor, as well as marriages, be made in heaven?———My Uncle Toby mused.———

Religion inclined him to say one thing, and his high idea of military skill tempted him to say another; so not being able to frame a reply exactly to his mind———my Uncle Toby said nothing at all. (p. 608)

Benevolence is never toppled from her throne within Uncle Toby, but she is constantly threatened, even in the story of Le Fever:

It was to my Uncle Toby's eternal honor,———though I tell it only for the sake of those, who, when cooped in betwixt a natural and a positive law [*i.e.*, between rational morality and revealed commands], know not for their souls, which way in the world to turn themselves———That notwithstanding my Uncle Toby was warmly engaged at that time in carrying on the siege of Dendermond, parallel with the allies, who pressed theirs on so vigorously, that they scarce allowed him time to get his dinner———that nevertheless he gave up Dendermond, though he had already made a lodgment upon the counterscarp;———and bent his whole thoughts towards the private distresses at the inn; and, except that he ordered the garden gate to be bolted up, by which he might be said to have turned the siege of Dendermond into a blockade,———he left Dendermond to itself,———to be relieved or not by the French king, as the French king thought good; and only considered how he himself should relieve the poor lieutenant and his son.

———That kind Being, who is friend to the friendless, shall recompense thee for this. (pp. 423-424)

Any decent person who has an overweening desire becomes a part of this moral comedy—a faithful family servant even, so long as she has a touch of madness for silk gowns. The seemingly innocent foible is the moral snag in Sterne's "dear creatures."

The method of the *Sentimental Journey* differs only slightly. The threat to Yorick's moral character is less obviously idiosyncratic. His sentimental hobby is hardly the harmless little filly ridden by Uncle Toby. His yearning for love and generosity and *politesse de coeur* represents a powerful desire felt by the world at large. Sterne shows us how the sentimental streak in each of us can become our moral *hamartia*. And the novel has a rational cast: if we are not critical, we misjudge the kindness of others; if we fail to see our own feelings of love and pity in terms larger than our immediate experience, if we do not refer our conduct to the eternal moral truths, we only flatter ourselves. The benevolism of the *Sentimental Journey* is no more didactic than the treatment of noses in *Tristram Shandy*, but the comedy is poignant and reaches all of us. For we all like to think of ourselves as generous and sympathetic and charitable to our fellows.

As a humorist, Sterne has the stature attributed to him by Jean Paul Richter, by Scherer, and Read. His laughter itself had greatness, said Jean Paul, for he looked down upon the small world of man from heights that are immortal. It would be overly simple to claim that Sterne's rational ethics, his concept of eternal, immutable moral truths, could by itself prove that he had such a noble humoristic point of view. Still, the sermons suggest the possibility. The vision of a cosmos of pure, abstract Reason, the great and perfect Reality above and independent of man, though known imperfectly by him, above and independent of any anthropomorphic deity, is indeed a noble vision. I do not mean to suggest that the dignity of the philosophy will necessarily be imparted to the character of the adherents. Not every rationalist achieves the courage and honesty and peace of a Socrates—and a humorist never. The humorist does not forget the disparity between what he knows and what he is. His own conduct is part of the foolish world at which he laughs. Hence the pain and melancholy in his laughter, remarked by Jean Paul. Corporal Trim is trying to elevate the thoughts of the servants in the kitchen by reminding them "we are not stocks and stones," when Sterne (cribbing from his own sermons) interposes,

> ——'tis very well. I should have added, nor are we angels, I wish we were,——but men clothed with bodies, and governed by our imaginations;——and what a junketing piece of work of it there is, betwixt these and our seven senses, especially some of them. . . . (p. 361)[2]

The least meritorious of Sterne's characters are his narrators, Tristram Shandy and Mr. Yorick, because they are the most aware and sensitive—men from whom high moral conduct might be expected. And these two have the names which Sterne assumed himself.

[2]Compare Sermon XLIII: "We are not angels, but men clothed with bodies, and, in some measure, governed by our imaginations. . . ." (Vol. II, p. 345).

Critics are sometimes careless in failing to distinguish between the man Sterne and his narrators, but their confusion was fostered by Sterne. He did not want to hold himself aloof like a wise teacher. If the narrator who is Tristram-Sterne-Yorick teaches as much folly as wisdom, he persuades us he believes the folly. When he pokes fun at our vanity, he frankly displays his own. He may make us snicker at a dirty joke, but he can hardly hide his own laughter. He can evoke our tears of pity, but he is not himself afraid to cry. Sterne draws us into his story as his companions and equals. Once there, we discover we are all fools. That is the lesson taught by all great humorists.

Humor, said Jean Paul, is like the mythical bird, Merops, which turns its tail toward Heaven, but manages, flying in that position, to get to Heaven. The world has looked upon Laurence Sterne as a bird with its tail toward Heaven. Too seldom has it noticed in which direction he flies.

AN APPENDIX ON
THE JOURNAL TO ELIZA

AN APPENDIX ON
THE JOURNAL TO ELIZA

Laurence Sterne experimented with one work of full-blown emotionalism, independent of rational restraints—the daybook to Eliza Draper which is now called *The Journal to Eliza*. Since this fragment was discovered a century ago by a boy of Bath playing in an old storeroom, it has become inseparably linked in the public mind with the *Sentimental Journey*—and with good reason, since in the novel Yorick openly addresses Eliza as his beloved. Mrs. Draper, an attractive matron of twenty-three, wife of an official of the East India Company, had come to England with her husband, but because of poor health had remained when Daniel Draper returned to India. Sterne met her in 1767 at the home of their mutual friends, the Jameses. They quickly formed a "sentimental attachment," exchanging letters and gifts, seeing one another in the company of friends. Despite their both being married, their friends generally approved this public flirtation. Nevertheless, Daniel Draper wrote his wife to return to India. Before parting, only three months after they had met, Eliza and Sterne agreed to write journals to each other which they would exchange upon their reunion. They never saw one another again. The major portion of Sterne's journal survives; Eliza's, if she ever wrote it, has been lost.[1]

The view popularized by Wilbur Cross, that the document reveals "the pathological state of the emotions—long suspected but never quite known to a certainty—whence springs the *Sentimental Journey*," was exploded by Rufus Putney's series of articles.[2] As I

[1] The account given by Cross, pp. 428-458, should be read along with Putney's corrective version.

[2] "The Evolution of *A Sentimental Journey*," *PQ*, XIX (1940), 349-369. "Sterne's Eliza," *TLS*, March 9, 1946, p. 115. "Alas, Poor Eliza!," *MLR*, XLI (1946), 411-413. "Laurence Sterne: Apostle of Laughter," *The Age of Johnson: Essays Presented to Chauncey Brewster Tinker* (Yale University Press), 1949, pp. 159-170.

have stated, I cannot subscribe to Putney's view of Sterne's sentimentalism as a "hoax," but his opinion that Sterne "mocked in the
Sentimental Journey the foolish figure he had cut with Eliza Draper"
cannot be doubted. Sterne was not deeply in love with Mrs. Draper,
but was consciously toying with the experiences and the literature of
the heart.

All parties admit that *The Journal to Eliza* was written as a public,
not private, epistle. Cross reports, "As if designed for publication,
the manuscript contains numerous blots and interlineations for better
phrases, in addition to the introductory note, which was clearly
framed to mystify the general reader." Flattered by the interest of a
young, handsome woman, Sterne must have enjoyed concocting a
literary chronicle which he fancied as a complement to the experience. But soon after Eliza's departure, Sterne fell ill; and a few weeks
later, he dragged a very weak frame north to Yorkshire. Putney has
pointed out, however, that Sterne's "normal" strength, such as that
was, soon returned. He soon settled down to work in his study at
Coxwold, with no more disturbing a companion at hand than his
cat. It was then, I believe, that Sterne's flirtation with Eliza Draper
and the journal he had written about it began to look very silly indeed.

A perusal of the historical evidence indicates that, while Sterne was
still in London and for a few weeks after he left, the *Journal* and the
Journey competed for his attention. He had been planning a new
novel half a year before he met Eliza, but he did not set to work on
it until March of 1767, at the height of his flirtation (*Letters*, pp.
284, 313). On April 12, a few days after the parting, he began the
epistle. He probably worked on both manuscripts during the next
six weeks, returning home in May. Near the end of that June, he appears to have decided he could not divide his time between them; at
least, as indicated by a letter of June 30, he was anxious about the
novel—"I ought to be busy from sunrise, to sun set, for I have a
book to write—a wife to receive—an estate to sell—a parish to super-
intend, and what is worst of all, a disquieted heart to reason with"
(*Letters*, p. 369). When he copied this remark into the daybook a
few days later (July 7), he used it as an excuse for not making longer
entries. That was the day after he had written to Mrs. James, "I am
now beginning to be truly busy at my Sentimental Journey—the pains
and sorrows of this life having retarded its progress" (*Letters*,

p. 375). But, as Putney shows, these pains and sorrows could not have been too destructive since Sterne broke off *The Journal to Eliza* on August 3 with a trumped-up excuse that his wife was returning, when he knew she was not due for a month. Thereafter, he worked rapidly on his novel (*Letters*, pp. 393, 395), not again taking up the *Journal* except for a final brief note of November 1. The report of Richard Griffith indicates the book was half completed in mid-September (*Letters*, pp. 398-399, n. 3), and by December 3 Sterne was calculating to finish by Christmas (*Letters*, p. 405). On February 27 the *Sentimental Journey* was published. It seems likely that Sterne decided his *Journal to Eliza* was not worth continuing—not, at least, if it interfered with his little novel.

In my opinion, Sterne realized, as do most readers today, that the daybook was an inferior work. Wilbur Cross and those who shared his view were led astray by an assumption that the two works emanated from the same sentimental animus. What strikes me is the remarkable difference between the two, the loose irrationality of the epistle to Eliza contrasting with the moral rationality which underpins the novel. In *The Journal to Eliza,* Sterne seems to forget or invert all the values which support the *Sentimental Journey.* The emphasis in the love letters is upon feeling alone, quite aside from the actions which give rise to them or result from them. Sterne writes about his loving regard for Eliza, his misery at their separation, his anticipation of their eventual reunion and marriage. The writing is maudlin and tasteless. He flaunts the account of his diseased genitals (pp. 329-330),[3] and blatantly wishes for the deaths of Daniel Draper and Mrs. Sterne (pp. 359, 366, 370-371). His craving for sentiments, which in the *Sentimental Journey* is comically set over against his duty, is here excused by a neurotic hedonism: "[I] begin to feel a pleasure in this kind of resigned misery arising from this situation, of heart unsupported by ought but its own tenderness" (p. 324). In the novel, Yorick too wants the pleasure of feeling "the movements which rise" out of desire, but he knows he must "govern them" as a good man (p. 173). Mr. Yorick is constantly tortured by self-doubt, but not so Sterne in *The Journal to Eliza*: "I trust all I have to it [love]

---

[3]Page references to *The Journal to Eliza* are to that edition included in Curtis's general edition of the *Letters.* For further comments upon Sterne's disease, see his letter to the Earl of Shelburne, pp. 342-344.

—as I trust Heaven, which *cannot leave me, without a fault, to perish"* (p. 351; italics mine).

Furthermore, there is no opposition between the head and the heart in the *Journal.* "Thou hast only turned the tide of my passions a new way," writes Sterne; "they flow, Eliza, to thee—and ebb from every other object in this world—and reason tells me they do right" (p. 323). "Thou art mistress, Eliza, of all the powers he [Sterne] has to soothe and protect thee—for thou art mistress of his heart; his affections; and his reason" (p. 357). In the published novel, Yorick never gives up his reason to his sentiments, least of all when women evoke the affection: when he is embarrassed at holding the hand of Madame de L***, the lady herself remarks on the conflict of heart and head—"the heart knew it [Yorick's wish], and was satisfied; and who but an English philosopher would have sent notice of it to the brain to reverse the judgment?" (p. 29).

The references to God in the two works show a remarkable contrast. In the *Sentimental Journey* Yorick's prayers, comic though they be, are prayers for moral strength (the one exception is immediately corrected by Yorick—p. 80) or for the welfare of others. Yorick may feel sexual desire for Maria at one moment and call upon God to protect her at the next (p. 217), but he is taking leave of the maid, and we cannot doubt his altruism. In *The Journal to Eliza*, Sterne's prayers are selfish and petty. He may ask Jesus for a "recompense for the sorrows and disappointments" Eliza has suffered, but he also wants himself to be "the instrument" (pp. 333-334). His ill-founded confidence that God will protect his and Eliza's interests, he guilelessly describes as a "religious elixir" (p. 337). And he is certain the deity has a special concern for this flirtation—"God made us not for misery and ruin—he has ordered all our steps—and influenced our attachments. . . . It must end well" (p. 352). Sterne even borrows a line from his sermons which originally had expressed his terror of God—"a Being about our paths and about our beds, whose omniscient eye spies out all our ways" [4]—to transform it into a description of Eliza's haunting spirit: "Thou shalt lie down and rise up with me—about my bed and about my paths, and shall see out all my ways" (p. 387).

[4]Sermon XXX, Vol. II, p. 159; a close self-plagiarism occurs in Sermon XXXIII, Vol. II, p. 208.

The Journal to Eliza is not a rationalistic work. It is not, for that matter, a moral work, for it sets aside all moral standards.

The document should be taken as evidence for the kind of weakness at which Sterne laughed in the *Sentimental Journey*. No doubt, Sterne himself had the weakness. To the *Journal* can be added the fragmentary evidences of numerous sentimental dalliances. Sterne "fell in love" easily, especially with young women in pathetic circumstances, such as the forlorn Huguenot concert-hall singer, Catherine Fourmantel—the "dear Jenny" of *Tristram Shandy*—or with young ladies of a fragile constitution such as Mrs. Draper or Sarah Tuting, who was ill in bed when she received Sterne's expressions of sympathy subtly mingled with hints of forbidden desires:

> The gentle Sally T—— is made up of too fine a texture for the rough wearing of the world—some gentle brother, or someone who sticks closer than a brother, should now take her by the hand, and lead her tenderly along her way—pick carefully out the smoothest tracks for her—scatter roses on them—and when the laxed and weary fiber tells him she is weary—take her up in his arms—
>
> I despise mankind, that not one of the race does this for her— You know what I have to say further—but adieu. (*Letters*, p. 224)

There can be little doubt Sterne transferred his amorous sentimentality into the *Sentimental Journey*. Madame de L*** herself might be modeled on Miss Tuting; or at least Yorick's feelings for the fitcional lady may be modeled upon Stern's feelings for the real one:

> Melancholy! to see such sprightliness the prey of sorrow.—I pitied her from my soul; and though it may seem ridiculous enough to a torpid heart,—I could have taken her into my arms, and cherished her, though it was in the open street, without blushing. (*Sentimental Journey*, pp. 30-31)

Sterne was conscious of his own tendency to spiritualize his feelings of concupiscence. In a letter to William Stanhope, he wrote about sensuality, ". . . you can feel! Aye so can my cat, when he hears a female caterwauling on the housetop—but caterwauling disgusts me.

I had rather raise a gentle flame, than have a different one raised in me" (*Letters*, p. 394). But notice that he does not say he wants no flame at all. The letter expresses in its own way what Sterne says in the *Sentimental Journey*—"L'amour n'est *rien* sans sentiment. Et le sentiment est encore *moins* sans amour." However, because Sterne used this facet of his personality as subject material for the novel, we need not jump to the conclusion that he had no critical, objective perspective on it. The digression upon Bevoriskius and the cocksparrow in the *Sentimental Journey* gives a seriocomical divine sanction to open animality. It suggests that a frank and lusty desire is more admirable than Yorick's sort of pruriency, which masks the sexual appetite out of feelings of shame:

> But there is nothing unmixed in this world; and some of the gravest of our divines have carried it so far as to affirm that enjoyment itself was attended even with a sigh—and the greatest *they knew* of terminated *in a general way*, in little better than a convulsion.
>
> I remember the grave and learned Bevoriskius, in his commentary upon the generations from Adam, very naturally breaks off in the middle of a note to give an account to the world of a couple of sparrows upon the out-edge of his window, which had incommoded him all the time he wrote, and, at last had entirely taken him off from his genealogy.
>
> —'Tis strange! writes Bevoriskius; but the facts are certain, for I have had the curiosity to mark them down one by one with my pen—but the cock-sparrow during the little time that I could have finished the other half this note, has actually interrupted me with the reiteration of his caresses three and twenty times and a half.
>
> How merciful, adds Bevoriskius, is heaven to his creatures!
>
> Ill fated Yorick! that the gravest of thy brethren should be able to write that to the world, which stains thy face with crimson to copy in even thy study.
>
> But this is nothing to my travels—So I twice—twice beg pardon for it. (pp. 162-163)[5]

[5]Sterne's joke about a learned divine who unconsciously revealed so much about his personal life, may refer to the former Archbishop of

It seems to me that anyone who would tell that story is not languishing in sentimental love, either for Madame de L*** or for Eliza Draper.

Of course Sterne wrote autobiographically. How can a writer do otherwise? He drew from his abundant experience as a flirt when writing both the *Journal* and the *Journey*, but the results differ. In *The Journal to Eliza* Sterne's amorous sentimentality is regarded as an end in itself. In the *Sentimental Journey* it is laughed at. Had Sterne been completely captivated by his love for Eliza Draper, had he thought that an effusion of emotions without the control of reason had any value, he would have abandoned the novel in order to complete *The Journal to Eliza*. Instead, he chose to be the humorist, to laugh at himself along with the rest of the world, to turn his own folly into a comedy of moral sentiments.

Cantebury, John Tillotson. In his seventh sermon Tillotson says, "None of the comforts of this life are pure and unmixed. There is something of *vanity* mingled with all our earthly enjoyments, and that causeth *vexation of spirit*"—*Works*, with a life by Thomas Birch (London, 1752), Vol. I, 72.

SELECTED BIBLIOGRAPHY

I

SEVENTEENTH- AND

EIGHTEENTH-CENTURY WORKS

Adams, William. *The Nature and Obligation of Virtue.* . . . London, 1754.

Balguy, John. *A Collection of Tracts, Moral and Theological.* . . . London, 1734.

[Bayes, Thomas]. *Divine Benevolence.* . . . London, 1731.

Burton, Robert. *Anatomy of Melancholy* (first published 1621), ed. Floyd Dell and Paul Jorden-Smith. New York, 1948.

Butler, Joseph. *Works*, ed. W[illiam] E[wart] Gladstone. 2 vols. Oxford, 1896.

[Campbell, Archibald]. *APETH-ΛOΓIA or, An Enquiry into the Original of Moral Virtue.* . . , pirated by and published under the name of Alexander Innes. Westminster, 1728.

Clarke, John [of Hull]. *An Examination of the Notion of Moral Good and Evil.* . . . London, 1725.

────────────. *The Foundation of Morality in Theory and Practice.* . . . York, n. d. [c. 1727].

Clarke, Samuel. *Works*, intro. Benjamin [Hoadly]. 4 vols. London, 1738.

────────────. *The Leibniz-Clarke Correspondence,* ed. H[enry] G[avin] Alexander. New York, 1956.

Cockburn, Catherine [née Trotter]. *The Works of Mrs. Catharine Cockburn.* . . , with a life by Thomas Birch. 2 vols. London, 1751.

Cumberland, Richard [Bishop of Peterborough]. *A Philosophical Enquiry into the Laws of Nature* . . . (first published 1672 as *De Legibus Naturae Disquisitio philosophica.* . .), trans. John Towers. Dublin, 1750.

Fiddes, Richard. *A General Treatise of Morality Form'd upon the Principles of Natural Reason. . . . London*, 1724.

Fielding, Henry. *The History of Tom Jones, a Foundling*. 6 vols. London, 1749.

Fordyce, David. *Dialogues Concerning Education*. 2 vols. London, 1745-48.

————. *Elements of Moral Philosophy* (first published in *The Preceptor*, ed. Robert Dodsley, Vol. II. London, 1748). London, 1754.

Gay, John [of Sidney College, Cambridge]. "Preliminary Dissertation Concerning the Fundamental Principle of Virtue or Morality," prefixed to *An Essay on the Origin of Evil. By Dr. William King. . .*, trans. Edmond Law. Cambridge, 1739.

[Glover, Philip]. *A Discourse Concerning Virtue and Religion. . . .* London, 1732.

Grotius, Hugo. *De Jure Belli ac Pacis*, Book III (first published 1625), trans. Francis W. Kelsey *et al.*, ed. James Brown Scott. Oxford and London, 1925.

Hartley, David. *Observations on Man . . .* (first published 1749). London, 1834.

Hobbes, Thomas. *Elements of Law, Natural and Politic* (first published 1650 as *Human Nature; or the Fundamental Elements of Policy. . .*, and, also 1650, *De Corpore Politico; the Elements of Law. . .*,) , ed. Ferdinand Tönnies. Cambridge, 1928.

————. *Leviathan . . .* (first published 1651), ed. Michael Oakeshott. Oxford, n. d.

Home, Henry, Lord Kames. *Elements of Criticism* (first published 1762), ed. James R. Boyd. New York, 1868.

Hume, David. *An Enquiry Concerning Human Understanding* (first published 1758) and *An Enquiry Concerning the Principles of Morals* (first published 1751), bound as one vol., ed. L[ewis] A[mherst] Selby-Bigge. Oxford, 1902.

————. *A Treatise of Human Nature* (first published 1739-40), ed. L[ewis] A[mherst] Selby-Bigge. Oxford, 1896.

Hutcheson, Francis. *An Essay on the Nature and Conduct of the Passions and Affections. With Illustrations on the Moral Sense.* London, 1728.

————. *Inquiry into the Original of our Ideas of Beauty and Virtue . . .* (first published 1725). London, 1738.

Jameson, William. *Essay on Virtue and Harmony.* ... Edinburgh, 1749.

Locke, John. *Essay Concerning Human Understanding* (first published 1690), ed. Alexander Campbell Fraser. Oxford, 1894.
—————. *Reasonableness of Christianity.* London, 1695.

[Long, James ?]. *An Enquiry into the Origin of the Human Appetites and Affections.* Lincoln, 1747 (re-issued in *Metaphysical Tracts by English Philosophers of the Eighteenth Century,* ed. Samuel Parr. London, 1837).

Mandeville, Bernard. *The Fable of the Bees: or, Private Vices, Publick Benefits* (first published 1705-23), ed. F[rederick] B[enjamin] Kaye. 2 vols. Oxford, 1924.
—————. *A Letter to Dion.* London, 1732 (The Augustan Reprint Society, No. 41, intro. Jacob Viner. Los Angeles, 1953).

Morris, Corbyn. *An Essay towards Fixing the True Standards of Wit, Humour, Raillery, Satire, and Ridicule.* ... London, 1744 (The Augustan Reprint Society, No. 4, intro. James L. Clifford. Los Angeles, 1947).

[Nettleton, Thomas]. *Some Thoughts Concerning Virtue and Happiness.* ... London, 1729.

Norris, John. *Practical Discourses upon the Beatitudes* ... (Vol. I of *Practical Discourses on Several Divine Subjects,* first published 1691-93). London, 1694.

Pope, Alexander. *Spectator,* No. 408 (Wednesday, June 18, 1712), in *Prose Works: Vol. I, The Earlier Works,* ed. Norman Ault. Oxford, 1936. Pp. 43-48.

Price, Richard. *A Review of the Principal Questions in Morals* (first published 1757), ed. D. Daiches Raphael. Oxford, 1948.

Rousseau, Jean Jacques. *Émile* (first published 1762), trans. Barbara Foxley. London and New York, 1911.

Rutherforth, T[homas]. *An Essay on the Nature and Obligation of Virtue.* Cambridge, 1744.

Shaftesbury, Anthony Ashley Cooper, Third Earl of. *Characteristics of Men, Manners, Opinions, Times* (first published 1711), ed. John M. Robertson. 2 vols. London, 1900.
—————. *Life, Unpublished Letters, and Philosophical Regimen.* ..., ed. Benjamin Rand. London and New York, 1900.

Smith, Adam. *Theory of Moral Sentiments* (first published 1759), with a memoir by Dugald Stewart. London, 1871.

Smollett, Tobias. *Travels through France and Italy* (first published 1766), intro. Thomas Seccombe. Oxford, 1919.

Sterne, Laurence. *The Life and Opinions of Tristram Shandy, Gentleman,* 1760-67. *A Sentimental Journey through France and Italy,* 1768. *Sermons of Mr. Yorick,* 1760-66. *Sermons by the Late Rev. Mr. Sterne,* 1769. *Letters,* 1773-75. *A Unique Catalogue of Laurence Sterne's Library* (facsimile reproduction with a preface by Charles Whibley, 1930). Page references are to the editions described in the prefatory note on documentation.

Stillingfleet, Edward. *Fifty Sermons Preached upon Several Occasions.* London, 1707.

[Sykes, Arthur Ashley]. *The True Foundations of Natural and Reveal'd Religion Asserted.* London, 1730.

Taylor, John [of Norwich]. *An Examination of the Scheme of Morality, Advanced by Dr. Hutcheson. . . .* London, 1759.

Tillotson, John. *Works,* with a life by Thomas Birch. 3 vols. London, 1752.

Tindal, Matthew. *Christianity as Old as the Creation. . . .* London, 1730.

Turnbull, George. *The Principles of Moral Philosophy. . . .* London, 1740.

Warburton, William. *The Divine Legation of Moses. . . ,* Vol. 1 [Books i-iii bound as one vol.], second edition (first published 1737-38). London, 1738.

Wollaston, William. *The Religion of Nature Delineated* (first published 1724), preface and trans. of notes [by John Clarke of Salisbury]. London, 1759.

II

NINETEENTH- AND

TWENTIETH-CENTURY WORKS

Aiken, Henry D. "Introduction," *Hume's Moral and Political Philosophy*. New York, 1948.

Albee, Ernest. "Clarke's Ethical Philosophy," Parts I, II, *Philosophical Review*, XXXVII (July and September, 1928), 304-327; 403-432.

Allen, Walter. *The English Novel: a Short Critical History*. New York, 1957.

Austin, E[ugene] M. *The Ethics of the Cambridge Platonists*. Philadelphia, 1935.

Baird, Theodore. "The Time-scheme of *Tristram Shandy* and a Source," *PMLA*, LI (September, 1936), 803-820.

Baker, Ernest A. *The History of the English Novel*. Vol. IV, *Intellectual Realism: from Richardson to Sterne*. London, 1930.

Birkhead, Edith. "Sentiment and Sensibility in the Eighteenth-Century Novel," *Essays and Studies by Members of the English Association*, XI (1925), 92-116.

Blanchard, Rae. "Introduction," *The Christian Hero by Richard Steele*. Oxford and London, 1932.

Bonar, James. *Moral Sense*. London and New York, 1930.

Booth, Wayne C. "Did Sterne Complete *Tristram Shandy?*" *Modern Philology*, XLVIII (February, 1951), 172-183.

——————. "The Self-Conscious Narrator in Comic Fiction before *Tristram Shandy*," *PMLA*, LXVII (March, 1952), 163-185.

Bredvold, Louis I. "The Invention of the Ethical Calculus," *The Seventeenth Century: Studies in the History of English Thought and Literature from Bacon to Pope, by Richard Foster Jones and Others Writing in his Honor*. Stanford, 1951, pp. 165-180.

147

Brett, R[aymond] L[aurence]. *The Third Earl of Shaftesbury: A Study in Eighteenth-Century Literary Theory*. London, 1951.

Broad, C[harlie] D[unbar]. *Five Types of Ethical Theory*. London, 1930.

Cash, Arthur H. "The Lockean Psychology of *Tristram Shandy*," *ELH*, XXII (June, 1955), 125-135.

——————. "The Sermon in *Tristram Shandy*," *ELH,* XXXI (December, 1964), 395-417.

Cazamian, Louis. *The Development of English Humor*. Durham, 1952.

Coleridge, Samuel Taylor. *Coleridge's Miscellaneous Criticism*, ed. Thomas Middleton Raysor. London, 1936.

Crane, R[onald] S. "Suggestions toward a Genealogy of the 'Man of Feeling,' " *ELH*, I (December, 1934), 205-230.

Cross, Wilbur L. *The Life and Times of Laurence Sterne*. New Haven, 1929.

Curtis, Lewis Perry. *The Politicks of Laurence Sterne*. Oxford and London, 1929.

Czerny, Johann. *Sterne, Hippel und Jean Paul*. Berlin, 1904.

De Pauley, W[illiam] C[ecil]. *The Candle of the Lord: Studies in the Cambridge Platonists*. London and New York, 1937.

Dilworth, Ernest Nevin. *The Unsentimental Journey of Laurence Sterne*. New York, 1948.

Erämetsä, Erik. *A Study of the Word 'Sentimental'.* . . . Helsinki, 1951.

Evans, A[rthur] W[illiam]. *Warburton and the Warburtonians: A Study of Some Eighteenth-Century Controversies*. Oxford and London, 1932.

Fluchère, Henri, *Laurence Sterne, de l'homme à l'oeuvre: Biographie critique et essai d'interprétation de 'Tristram Shandy.'* Paris [1961].

Fowler, Thomas. *Shaftesbury and Hutcheson*. New York, 1883.

Frankena, William. "Hutcheson's Moral Sense Theory," *Journal of the History of Ideas*, XVI (June, 1955), 356-375.

Fredman, Alice Green. *Diderot and Sterne*. New York, 1955.

Freud, Sigmund. *Beyond the Pleasure Principle*, in Vol. XVIII, and *Civilization and Its Discontents*, Vol. XXI, of *Standard Edition . . . Psychological Works*, gen. ed. James Strachey. London, 1955-61.

Hammond, Lansing Van der Heyden. *Laurence Sterne's 'Sermons of Mr. Yorick.'* New Haven, 1948.

Hazlitt, William. *Lectures on the Comic Writers*, Vol. VI, and *Contributions to the 'Edinburgh Review,'* Vol. XVI, of *Works*, ed.

P[ercival] P[resland] Howe. London and Toronto, 1930-34.

"The Head and the Heart." Anon. review, *Times Literary Supplement*, April 9, 1949, p. 232.

Holland, Norman N. "The Laughter of Laurence Sterne," *Hudson Review*, IX (Autumn, 1956), 422-430.

Howes, Alan B. *Yorick and the Critics: Sterne's Reputation in England, 1760-1868*. New Haven, 1958.

Hooker, E[dward] N[iles]. "Humor in the Age of Pope," *Huntington Library Quarterly*, XI (August, 1948), 361-385.

——————————. "Pope on Wit: The *Essay on Criticism*," *The Seventeenth Century: Studies in the History of English Thought and Literature from Bacon to Pope, by Richard Foster Jones and Others Writing in his Honor*. Stanford, 1951, pp. 225-246.

Hoopes, Robert. *Right Reason in the English Renaissance*. Cambridge, 1962.

Jefferson, D[ouglas] W[illiam]. *Laurence Sterne*. London, 1954.

——————————. "*Tristram Shandy* and the Tradition of Learned Wit," *Essays in Criticism*, I (July, 1951), 225-248.

Laird, John. *Hume's Philosophy of Human Nature*. London, 1932.

——————. *Philosophical Incursions into English Literature*. Cambridge, 1946.

Lehman, B[enjamin] H[arrison]. "Of Time, Personality, and the Author: a Study of *Tristram Shandy*," *University of California Studies in English*, VIII (1941), 233-250.

Lovejoy, Arthur O. *Essays in the History of Ideas*. Baltimore, 1948.

Maack, Rudolf. *Laurence Sterne im Lichte seiner Zeit*. Hamburg, 1936.

McKillop, Alan Dugald. *The Early Masters of English Fiction*. Lawrence, 1956.

——————————. "The Reinterpretation of Laurence Sterne," *Études Anglaises*, VII (January, 1954), 36-47.

MacLean, Kenneth. "Imagination and Sympathy: Sterne and Adam Smith," *Journal of the History of Ideas*, X (June, 1949), 399-410.

——————————. *John Locke and English Literature of the Eighteenth Century*. New Haven, 1936.

Martineau, James. *Types of Ethical Theory*. 2 vols. Oxford, 1891.

Mendilow, A[dam] A[braham]. *Time and the Novel*. London and New York, 1952.

Merwin, H[enry] C[hilds]. "Philosophy in Sterne," *Atlantic Monthly*, LXXIV (October, 1894), 521-527.

Monk, Samuel Holt. "Introduction," *Tristram Shandy*. . . . New York and Toronto, 1950.

More, Paul Elmer. *Shelburne Essays: Third Series*. Boston and New York, 1921.

Muir, Edwin. *Essays on Literature and Society*. London, 1949.

Muirhead, John H. *The Platonic Tradition in Anglo-Saxon Philosophy: Studies in the History of Idealism in England and America*. London and New York, 1931.

Ollard, S[idney] L[eslie]. "Sterne as a Parish Priest," *Times Literary Supplement*, May 25, 1933, p. 364; self-correction, June 1, 1933, p. 380.

—————————. "Sterne as a Young Parish Priest," *Times Literary Supplement*, March 18, 1926, p. 217.

Parish, Charles. *Twentieth-Century Criticism of Form in 'Tristram Shandy.'* Unpublished Ph. D. dissertation, University of New Mexico, 1959.

—————————. "The Nature of Mr. Tristram Shandy, Author," *Boston University Studies in English*, V (Summer, 1961), 74-90.

Piper, William Bowman. "Tristram Shandy's Digressive Artistry," *Studies in English Literature, 1500-1900*, I (Summer, 1961), 65-76.

—————————. "Tristram Shandy's Tragicomical Testimony," *Criticism*, III (Summer, 1961), 171-185.

Pottle, Frederick A. "Bozzy and Yorick," *Blackwood's Magazine*, CCXVII (March, 1925), 297-313.

Powicke, Frederick J. *The Cambridge Platonists*. . . . London and Toronto, 1926.

Priestley, J[ohn] B[oynton]. *The English Comic Characters*. London, 1937.

—————————. *English Humor*. London, New York, and Toronto, 1929.

Prior, Arthur N. *Logic and the Basis of Ethics*. Oxford, 1949.

Putney, Rufus D. S. "Alas Poor Eliza!" *Modern Language Review*, XLI (October, 1946) 411-413.

—————————. "The Evolution of *A Sentimental Journey*," *Philological Quarterly*, XIX (October, 1940), 349-369.

—————————. "Laurence Sterne: Apostle of Laughter," *The Age of Johnson: Essays Presented to Chauncey Brewster Tinker*. New Haven, 1949, pp. 159-170.

_____. "Sterne's Eliza," *Times Literary Supplement*, March 9, 1946, p. 115.

Quennell, Peter. *The Profane Virtues. Four Studies of the Eighteenth Century*. New York, 1945.

Raphael, D. Daiches. *The Moral Sense*. Oxford and London, 1947.

Read, Herbert. "Introduction," *A Sentimental Journey*. . . . London, 1929.

_____. *Collected Essays in Literary Criticism*. London, 1938.

Reid, Ben. "The Sad Hilarity of Sterne," *Virginia Quarterly Review*, XXXII (Winter, 1956), 107-130.

Richter, Jean Paul. *Vorschule der Aesthetik* (Abt. I, Bd. 11, *Jean Pauls Sämtliche Werke*). Weimer, 1935.

Scherer, Edmond. *Essays on English Literature*, trans. George Saintsbury. New York, 1891.

Scott, William Robert. *Francis Hutcheson, His Life, Teaching, and Position in the History of Philosophy*. Cambridge, 1900.

Selby-Bigge, L[ewis] A[mherst]. "Introduction," *The British Moralists*. 2 vols. Oxford, 1897.

Shackford, John B. "Sterne's Use of Catachresis in *Tristram Shandy*," *Iowa English Yearbook*, VI (Fall, 1963), 74-79.

Shaw, Margaret R.B. *Laurence Sterne: the Making of A Humorist, 1713-1762*. London, 1957.

Shepperson, Archibald Bolling. "Yorick as Ministering Angel," *Virginia Quarterly Review*, XXX (Winter, 1954), 54-66.

Stedmond, J[ohn] M[itchell]. "Genre and *Tristram Shandy*," *Philological Quarterly*, XXXVIII (October, 1959), 37-51.

Stephen, Leslie. *History of English Thought in the Eighteenth Century*. 2 vols. London, 1876.

Stout, Gardner Dominick. *Laurence Sterne: 'A Sentimental Journey through France and Italy,' by Mr. Yorick*. Edited with an Introduction and Notes. Unpublished Ph. D. dissertation, Stanford University, 1962.

_____. "Yorick's *Sentimental Journey*: a Comic 'Pilgrim's Progress' for the Man of Feeling," *ELH*, XXX (December, 1963), 395-412.

Swabey, William Curtis. *Ethical Theory from Hobbes to Kant*. New York, 1961.

Thackeray, W[illiam] M[akepeace]. *The English Humourists of the Eighteenth Century*. New York, 1900.

Towers, A[ugustus] R[obert]. "Sterne's Cock and Bull Story," *ELH*, XXIV (March, 1957), 12-29.

Traugott, John. *Tristram Shandy's World: Sterne's Philosophical Rhetoric*. Berkeley and Los Angeles, 1954.

Trilling, Lionel. *The Liberal Imagination: Essays on Literature and Society*. New York, 1950.

Tullock, John. *Rational Theology and Christian Philosophy in England in the Seventeenth Century*. 2 vols. Edinburgh and London, 1874.

Van Ghent, Dorothy. *English Novel, Form and Function*. New York, 1953.

Warren, Howard C. *A History of the Association Psychology*. New York, Chicago, and Boston, 1921.

Watkins, W[alter] B[aker] C[ritz]. *Perilous Balance: the Tragic Genius of Swift, Johnson, and Sterne*. Princeton, 1939.

Watt, Ian. *The Rise of the Novel: Studies in Defoe, Richardson and Fielding*. London, 1957.

Whewell, William. *Lectures on the History of Moral Philosophy*. Cambridge and London, 1862.

Woolf, Virginia. *Granite and Rainbow*. New York, 1958.

————————. *The Second Common Reader*. New York, 1932.